THE
Ultimate
SPANISH-ENGLISH
Picture Dictionary

written by Catherine Bruzzone & Vicky Barker

illustrated by Vicky Barker

Spanish advisors: Nicolás Olucha Sánchez & Rosi Perea

B.E.S.
PUBLISHING

First edition for the United States, its Dependencies, Canada, and the Philippines published in 2021 by B.E.S. Publishing
© Copyright 2021 by b small publishing, East Horsley, UK. All rights reserved. No part of this publication may be reproduced or distributed in any form or by any means without the written permission of the copyright owner.
All inquiries should be addressed to: Peterson's Publishing, LLC, 4380 S. Syracuse Street, Suite 200, Denver, CO 80237-2624
www.petersonsbooks.com
ISBN-13: 978-1-4380-8949-2
Date of Manufacture: January 2021   Manufactured by: WKT, Shenzhen, Guangdong, China   Printed in China   1 2 3 4 5
Library of Congress Control No applied for

Contents - Índice

een-dee-seh

hello
buenos días
bway-noss dee-ass

Words and phrases - Las palabras y las frases

lass pa-_lab_-rass ee lass _frah_-sess

Essential words   Palabras esenciales

Word list   85-96   Lista de palabras

There are four words for "the" in Spanish:
el la los las
"el" is for a masculine noun, singular
"la" is for a feminine noun, singular
"los" is for a masculine noun, plural
"las" is for a feminine noun, plural

In Spanish, nouns are either masculine or feminine. The word for giraffe is feminine (la jirafa/las jirafas) and the word for tiger is masculine (el tigre/los tigres). This does not mean that every giraffe is a girl and every tiger is a boy! It does affect how you spell adjectives describing them. See page 70.

At home - En casa

en <u>kah</u>-sa

door
la puerta
la <u>pwair</u>ta

window
la ventana
la ben<u>tah</u>-na

curtains
las cortinas
lass kor-<u>teen</u>-ass

sofa
el sofá
el sof-<u>a</u>

armchair
el sillón
el see-<u>yon</u>

cushion
el cojín
el koh<u>een</u>

picture
el cuadro
el <u>kwa</u>-dro

television
el televisor
el teh-leh-vee-<u>sohr</u>

phone
el teléfono
el teh-<u>leh</u>-fono

4

Kitchen - La cocina
la ko-<u>see</u>-na

sink
el fregadero
el frega-d<u>air</u>-o

refrigerator
el refrigerador
el reh-free-heh-rah-<u>dohr</u>

stove
el estufa
el es-<u>too</u>-fah

oven
el horno
el <u>or</u>-no

frying pan
la sartén para freír
la sar-<u>ten</u> para freh-<u>eer</u>

saucepan
la cacerola
la kaseh-<u>ro</u>-la

washing machine
la lavadora
la lavah-<u>dora</u>

apron
el delantal
el deh-lan-<u>tal</u>

kettle
el hervidor
el air-<u>bee</u>-dor

Setting the table - Poniendo la mesa

knife
el cuchillo
el koo<u>chee</u>-yo

spoon
la cuchara
la koo<u>char</u>-a

fork
el tenedor
el teneh-<u>dor</u>

plate
el plato
el <u>plah</u>-toh

glass
el vaso
el <u>bah</u>-so

teapot
la tetera
la teh-<u>taira</u>

cup
la taza
la <u>tas</u>-a

saucer
el platillo
el plat-<u>ee</u>-yo

bowl
el tazón
el tas-<u>on</u>

6

Breakfast time - La hora del desayuno

la <u>o</u>ra del dess-a-<u>yoo</u>no

table
la mesa
la <u>meh</u>-ssa

stool
el taburete
el taboo-<u>reh</u>-teh

pitcher
la jarra
la <u>hah</u>-ra

cereal
el cereal
el sair-eh-<u>al</u>

honey
la miel
la m<u>ee</u>-yel

juice
el jugo
el <u>hoo</u>-go

jam
la mermelada
la mairmeh-<u>lah</u>-da

toast
la tostada
la tost-<u>ah</u>-da

breakfast
el desayuno
el dess-a-<u>yoo</u>no

7

Bedroom - La habitación
la abeeta-see-<u>yon</u>

bed
la cama
la <u>kah</u>-ma

chest of drawers
la cómoda
la <u>kom</u>-oda

drawer
el cajón
el ka-<u>hon</u>

armoire
el armario
el ar-<u>mah</u>-reeyo

coat hanger
la percha
la <u>pair</u>-cha

alarm clock
el despertador
el despairta-<u>dor</u>

shelf
el estante
el est<u>an</u>-teh

rug
la alfombra
la al-<u>fom</u>-bra

light
la luz
la loos

8

Good night, sweet dreams - Buenas noches, dulces sueños

bway-nass nochess dool-sehs swen-yoss

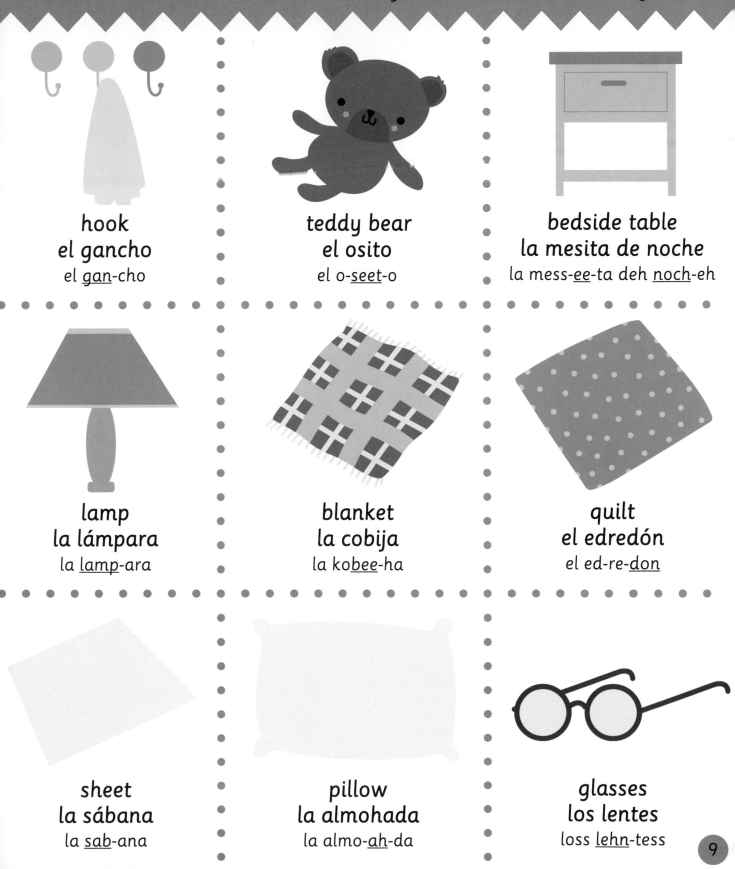

hook
el gancho
el gan-cho

teddy bear
el osito
el o-seet-o

bedside table
la mesita de noche
la mess-ee-ta deh noch-eh

lamp
la lámpara
la lamp-ara

blanket
la cobija
la kobee-ha

quilt
el edredón
el ed-re-don

sheet
la sábana
la sab-ana

pillow
la almohada
la almo-ah-da

glasses
los lentes
loss lehn-tess

9

Bathroom - El cuarto de baño

el <u>kwar</u>-toh deh <u>ban</u>-yo

sink
el lavamanos
el la-bah-<u>mah</u>-noss

toilet
el inodoro
el eeh-noh-<u>doh</u>-roh

toilet paper
el papél higiénico
el pa<u>pel</u> ee<u>hee</u>-en-eeko

shower
la ducha
la <u>doo</u>cha

bathtub
la bañera
la ban<u>yair</u>-a

faucet
el grifo
el <u>gree</u>-foh

water
el agua
el <u>ag</u>-wa

towel
la toalla
la toh-<u>ah</u>-ya

mirror
el espejo
el es<u>peh</u>-ho

Wash your hands! - ¡Lávate las manos!

la-bah-teh lass mah-noss

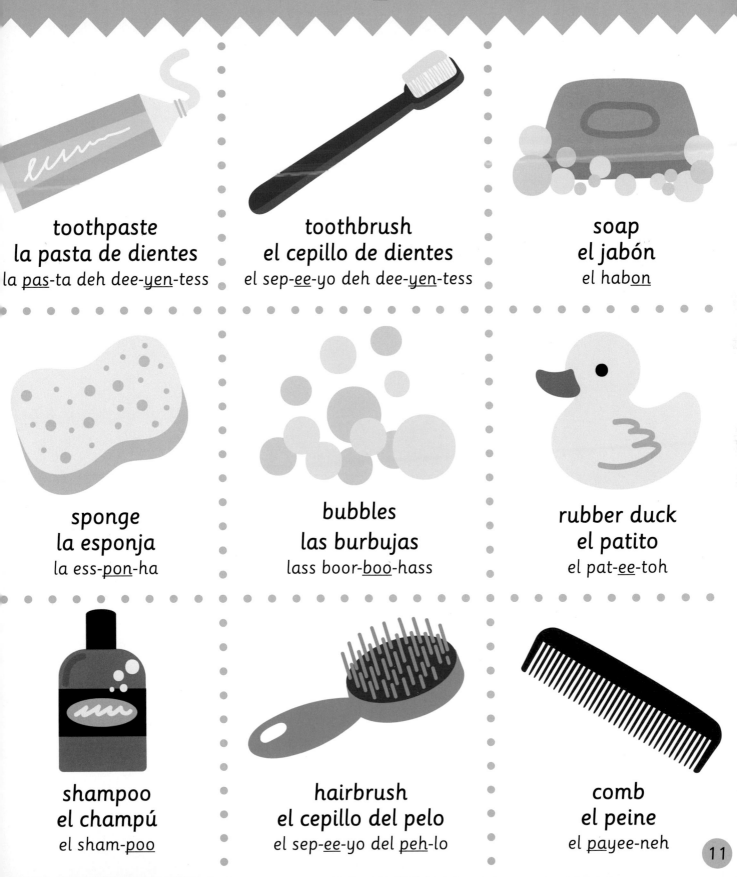

toothpaste
la pasta de dientes
la pas-ta deh dee-yen-tess

toothbrush
el cepillo de dientes
el sep-ee-yo deh dee-yen-tess

soap
el jabón
el habon

sponge
la esponja
la ess-pon-ha

bubbles
las burbujas
lass boor-boo-hass

rubber duck
el patito
el pat-ee-toh

shampoo
el champú
el sham-poo

hairbrush
el cepillo del pelo
el sep-ee-yo del peh-lo

comb
el peine
el payee-neh

11

Clothes - La ropa
la <u>ro</u>-pa

skirt
la falda
la <u>fal</u>-da

dress
el vestido
el bess-<u>tee</u>do

cardigan
el cárdigan
el kar-<u>dee</u>-gan

pants
los pantalones
loss panta-<u>lon</u>-ess

shirt
la camisa
la kam-<u>ee</u>-sa

tie
la corbata
la kor-<u>bah</u>-ta

coat
el abrigo
el ab<u>ree</u>-go

shoes
los zapatos
loss sapah-toss

socks
los calcetines
loss kalseh-<u>tee</u>-ness

What are you wearing today? - ¿Qué llevas hoy?

keh <u>yeh</u>-bass oy

T-shirt
la camiseta
la kah-mee-<u>seh</u>-ta

shorts
los pantalones cortos
loss panta-<u>lon</u>-ess <u>kor</u>-toss

sweater
el suéter
el <u>swet</u>-air

cap
la gorra
la <u>gor</u>-rah

boots
las botas
lass <u>boh</u>-tass

sneakers
las zapatillas
lass sapah-<u>tee</u>-yass

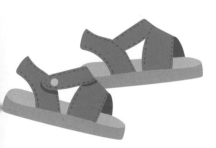

sandals
las sandalias
lass san<u>dal</u>-ee-ass

undershirt
la camiseta interior
la kah-mee-<u>seh</u>-ta een-teh-<u>reeor</u>

pajamas
el pijama
el pee<u>hah</u>-ma

13

Head and body - La cabeza y el cuerpo

la ka<u>beh</u>-sa ee el <u>kwair</u>-po

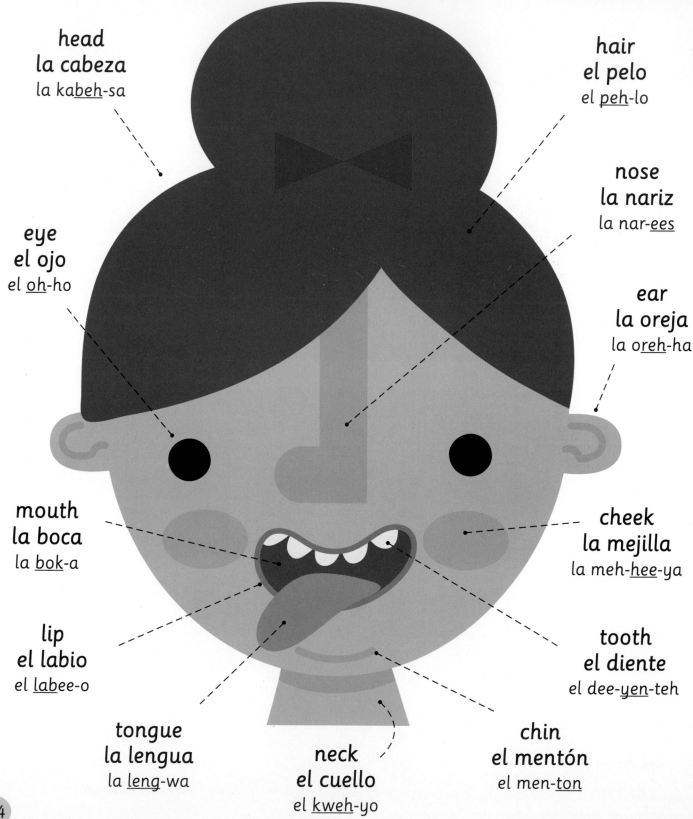

head
la cabeza
la ka<u>beh</u>-sa

hair
el pelo
el <u>peh</u>-lo

nose
la nariz
la nar-<u>ees</u>

eye
el ojo
el <u>oh</u>-ho

ear
la oreja
la o<u>reh</u>-ha

mouth
la boca
la <u>bok</u>-a

cheek
la mejilla
la meh-<u>hee</u>-ya

lip
el labio
el <u>labee</u>-o

tooth
el diente
el dee-<u>yen</u>-teh

tongue
la lengua
la <u>leng</u>-wa

neck
el cuello
el <u>kweh</u>-yo

chin
el mentón
el men-<u>ton</u>

14

Let's find... - Encontremos...

en-kon-<u>treh</u>-moss

shoulder
el hombro
el <u>om</u>bro

chest
el pecho
el <u>pech</u>-o

elbow
el codo
el <u>koh</u>-doh

finger
el dedo
el <u>deh</u>-doh

thumb
el pulgar
el pool-<u>gar</u>

foot
el pie
el pee-<u>yeh</u>

toe
el dedo
el <u>deh</u>-doh

hand
la mano
la <u>mah</u>-no

arm
el brazo
el <u>brah</u>-so

back
la espalda
la ess-<u>pal</u>-da

stomach
la barriga
la bar-<u>ee</u>-ga

leg
la pierna
la pee-<u>yair</u>na

knee
la rodilla
la rod<u>ee</u>-ya

nail
la uña
la <u>oon</u>-ya

15

Hospital - El hospital

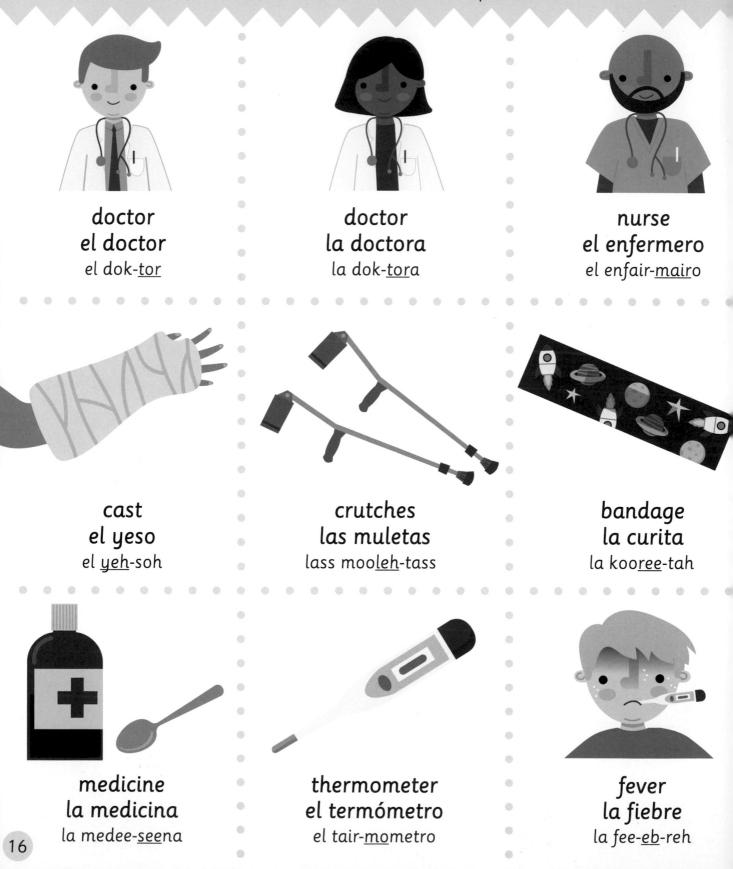

doctor
el doctor
el dok-<u>tor</u>

doctor
la doctora
la dok-<u>tora</u>

nurse
el enfermero
el enfair-<u>mairo</u>

cast
el yeso
el <u>yeh</u>-soh

crutches
las muletas
lass moo<u>leh</u>-tass

bandage
la curita
la koo<u>ree</u>-tah

medicine
la medicina
la medee-<u>seena</u>

thermometer
el termómetro
el tair-<u>mo</u>metro

fever
la fiebre
la fee-<u>eb</u>-reh

16

Ouch! Does it hurt? - ¡Ay! ¿Eso duele?
ay ess-o dweh-leh

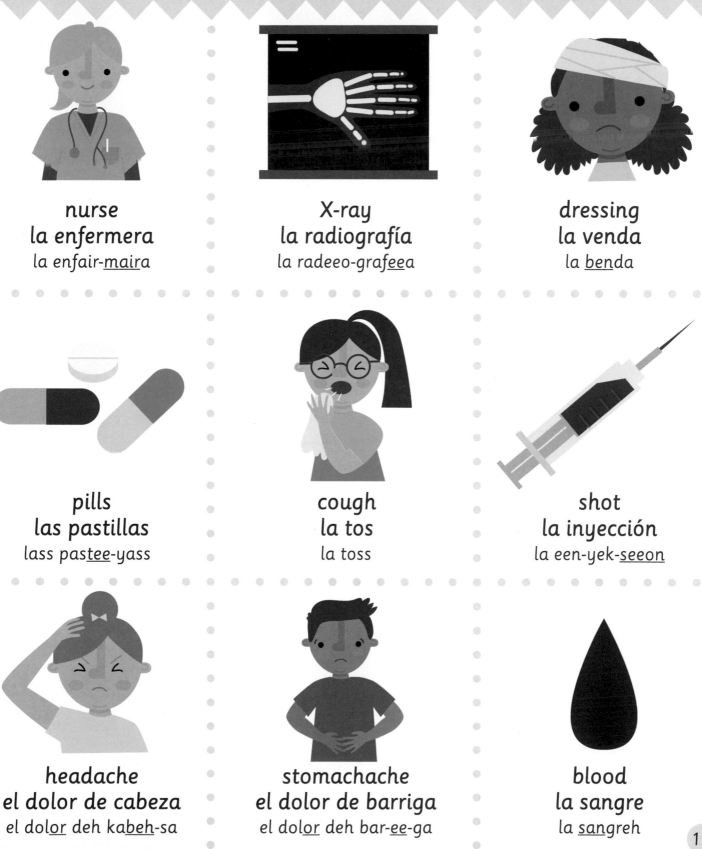

nurse
la enfermera
la enfair-maira

X-ray
la radiografía
la radeeo-grafeea

dressing
la venda
la benda

pills
las pastillas
lass pastee-yass

cough
la tos
la toss

shot
la inyección
la een-yek-seeon

headache
el dolor de cabeza
el dolor deh kabeh-sa

stomachache
el dolor de barriga
el dolor deh bar-ee-ga

blood
la sangre
la sangreh

17

Farm animals - Los animales de la granja

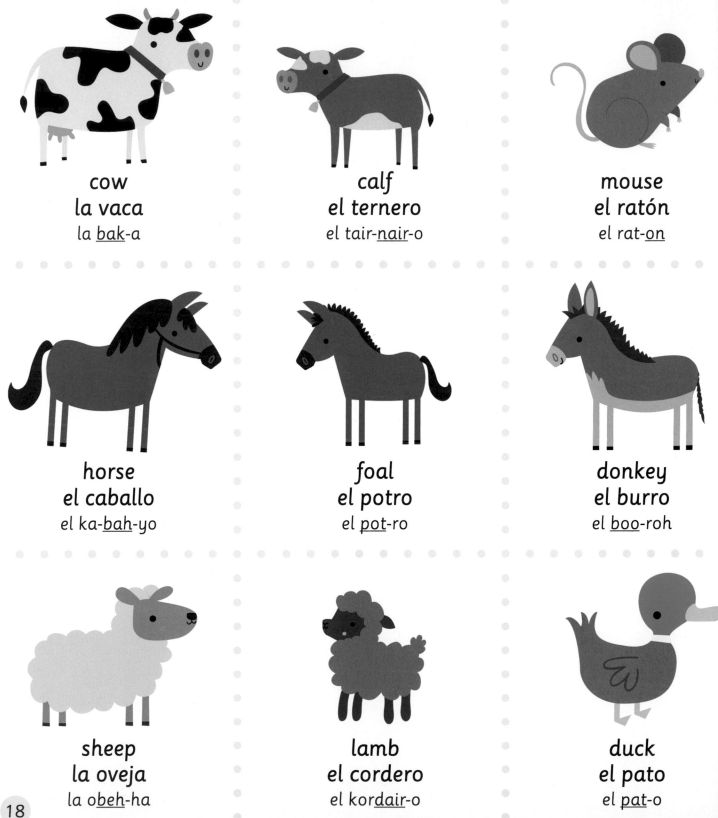

cow
la vaca
la <u>bak</u>-a

calf
el ternero
el tair-<u>nair</u>-o

mouse
el ratón
el rat-<u>on</u>

horse
el caballo
el ka-<u>bah</u>-yo

foal
el potro
el <u>pot</u>-ro

donkey
el burro
el <u>boo</u>-roh

sheep
la oveja
la o<u>beh</u>-ha

lamb
el cordero
el kor<u>dair</u>-o

duck
el pato
el <u>pat</u>-o

18

Which animals say "quack"? - ¿Qué animales dicen "cua"?

ke anee-_mah_-lehs _dee_-sehn kua

rooster
el gallo
el _gah_-yo

hen
la gallina
la ga-_yeen_-a

chick
el pollito
el po_yeet_-o

pig
el cerdo
el _saird_-o

piglet
el cerdito
el sair-_deet_-o

goat
la cabra
la _kab_-ra

duckling
el patito
el pa_teet_-o

goose
el ganso
el _gan_-so

gosling
el ansarino
el ansah-_ree_-no

Wild animals - Los animales salvajes

loss anee-<u>mah</u>-less sal<u>vah</u>-hess

giraffe
la jirafa
la hee-<u>rah</u>-fa

hippopotamus
el hipopótamo
el eepo-<u>pot</u>-tam-o

tiger
el tigre
el <u>tee</u>-greh

monkey
el mono
el <u>mon</u>-o

polar bear
el oso polar
el <u>oh</u>-so pol-<u>lar</u>

lion
el león
el leh-<u>on</u>

elephant
el elefante
el eleh-<u>fan</u>-teh

crocodile
el cocodrilo
el kokko-<u>dree</u>-lo

gorilla
el gorila
el go-<u>ree</u>-la

Can you see an animal with stripes? - ¿Puedes ver un animal con rayas?

pway-dess bair oon anee-mal kon rah-yass

kangaroo
el canguro
el kahn-goo-roh

brown bear
el oso pardo
el oh-so par-doh

koala
el koala
el koh-ah-la

rhinoceros
el rinoceronte
el reeno-sairon-teh

panda
el panda
el pan-da

chameleon
el camaleón
el kamal-eh-on

zebra
la cebra
la seb-ra

bat
el murciélago
el moor-see-eh-lago

meerkat
el suricato
el sooree-kah-toh

21

Pets - Las mascotas

lass mas<u>kot</u>-ass

cat
el gato
el <u>gat</u>-o

kitten
el gatito
el gat-<u>eet</u>-o

hamster
el hámster
el <u>am</u>-stair

dog
el perro
el <u>pehr</u>-ro

puppy
el cachorro
el ka<u>chor</u>-ro

parrot
el papagayo
el papa-<u>gah</u>-yo

lizard
el lagarto
el la<u>gar</u>-toh

snake
la serpiente
la sairp-<u>yen</u>-teh

guinea pig
el conejillo de indias
el koneh-<u>heey</u>o deh
<u>een</u>dee-ass

22

Birds - Los pájaros
loss <u>pa</u>-ha-ross

ostrich
el avestruz
el av-ehs-<u>troos</u>

swan
el cisne
el <u>siz</u>-neh

flamingo
el flamenco
el flam-<u>en</u>-ko

swallow
la golondrina
la golon-<u>dreen</u>-a

penguin
el pingüino
el peen-<u>gween</u>-o

owl
el búho
el <u>boo</u>-oh

eagle
el águila
el <u>ag</u>-ee-la

pelican
el pelícano
el pel-<u>ee</u>-kano

peacock
el pavo
el <u>pah</u>-bo

23

Camping - El camping

el <u>kamp</u>-ing

tent
la tienda de campaña
la <u>tyeen</u>-da deh kam-<u>pan</u>-ya

sleeping bag
el saco de dormir
el <u>sah</u>-ko deh dor-<u>meer</u>

camping chair
la silla de camping
la <u>see</u>-ya deh <u>kamp</u>-ing

campfire
la fogata
la foh-<u>gah</u>-ta

mug
la taza
la <u>tas</u>-a

map
el mapa
el <u>mah</u>-pa

compass
la brújula
la <u>broo</u>-hoo-la

flashlight
la linterna
la leen-<u>tair</u>-na

hammock
la hamaca
la am-<u>ah</u>-ka

Flowers - Las flores
lass flor-ess

daisy
la margarita
la marga-reet-a

daffodil
el narciso
el nar-see-so

rose
la rosa
la rosa

buttercup
el botón de oro
el bo-ton deh o-ro

bluebell
la campanilla
la kampan-ee-ya

lily
el lirio
el lee-ree-o

dandelion
el diente de león
el dee-yen-teh deh lay-on

snowdrop
la campanilla de invierno
la kampan-ee-ya deh
een-bee-air-no

tulip
el tulipán
el toolee-pan

Family - La familia
la fam-*eel*-ya

grandfather
el abuelo
el ab*weh*-lo

grandmother
la abuela
la ab*weh*-la

mother/mommy
la madre/mamá
la *mah*-dreh/ma*ma*

father/daddy
el padre/papá
el *pah*-dreh/pa*pa*

brother
el hermano
el air*mah*-no

sister
la hermana
la air*mah*-na

26

Here is... - Aquí está...
ess-<u>ta</u>

aunt
la tía
la <u>tee</u>-ya

uncle
el tío
el <u>tee</u>-yo

nephew
el sobrino
el sob-<u>ree</u>-no

cousin
el primo
el <u>pree</u>-mo

niece
la sobrina
la sob-<u>ree</u>-na

cousin
la prima
la <u>pree</u>-ma

grandson
el nieto
el nee-<u>eh</u>-toh

granddaughter
la nieta
la nee-<u>eh</u>-ta

27

Playground - El parque infantil
el <u>par</u>-keh eenfan-<u>teel</u>

swing
el columpio
el kol-<u>oom</u>-pee-o

seesaw
el subibaja
el soobee-<u>ba</u>ha

slide
el tobogán
el tobo-<u>gan</u>

sandbox
el cajón de arena
el ka-<u>hon</u> deh ah-<u>rayna</u>

jungle gym
el pasamanos
el pass-ah-<u>mah</u>-noss

tunnel
el túnel
el <u>too</u>-nel

bench
el banco
el <u>ban</u>-ko

path
el camino
el kam-<u>een</u>-o

picnic
el picnic
el <u>peek</u>-neek

Park - El parque
el par-keh

grass
la hierba
la yair-ba

pond
el estanque
el ess-tan-keh

stepping stones
el camino de piedras
el kam-ee-no deh
pee-ed-rass

tree
el árbol
el ar-bol

rowboat
el bote de remos
el boh-teh deh reh-moss

oar
el remo
el reh-mo

bush
el arbusto
el ar-boo-sto

fountain
la fuente
la foo-en-teh

snack bar
la cafetería
la kafeh-tair-ee-ya

29

Toys - Los juguetes
loss hoo<u>geht</u>-ess

kite
la cometa
la koh-<u>meh</u>-ta

robot
el robot
el ro-<u>bot</u>

ball
la pelota
la peh-<u>lot</u>-a

jigsaw puzzle
el rompecabezas
el rompeh-ka<u>beh</u>-sass

toy train
el trenecito de juguete
el treneh-<u>seet</u>-o deh
hoo<u>geht</u>-eh

doll
la muñeca
la moon-<u>yeh</u>-ka

paints
las pinturas
lass peen-<u>too</u>-rass

paintbrush
el pincel
el peen-<u>sell</u>

magic set
el juego de magia
el <u>hweh</u>-go deh <u>maheea</u>

drum
el tambor
el tam-<u>bor</u>

costume
el disfraz
el deess-<u>fras</u>

book
el libro
el <u>lee</u>-bro

puppet
el títere
el <u>teet</u>-eh-reh

guitar
la guitarra
la gee<u>tar</u>-ra

skateboard
la patineta
la pah-teen-<u>eh</u>-ta

xylophone
el xilófono
el see-<u>lo</u>-fono

blocks
los bloques
loss <u>blok</u>-ess

dinosaur
el dinosaurio
el dee-noh-<u>sahw</u>-reeo

31

Party - La fiesta
la fee-ess-ta

decorations
la decoración
la deh-kor-ah-see-yon

cake
el pastel
el pas-tel

candle
la vela
la beh-la

ice cream
el helado
el el-ah-doh

sandwich
el sándwich
el sand-weech

chocolate
el chocolate
el chokko-lah-teh

pizza
la pizza
la peet-za

french fries
las papas fritas
lass pah-pas free-tass

milkshake
el batido
el bat-ee-doh

When is your birthday? - ¿Cuándo es tu cumpleaños?

kwan-doh ess too koompleh-anyoss

games
los juegos
loss hweh-goss

party dress
el vestido de fiesta
el bes-teedo deh fee-ess-ta

cupcakes
las magdalenas
lass magda-leh-nass

balloon
el globo
el gloh-boh

party hat
el sombrero de fiesta
el som-brairo deh fee-ess-ta

music
la música
la moo-see-ka

magic wand
la varita mágica
la baree-ta ma-heeka

Happy birthday!
¡Feliz cumpleaños!
fel-ees koompleh-anyoss

present
el regalo
el reg-ah-lo

Telling stories - Los cuentos

loss <u>kwen</u>-toss

dragon
el dragón
el drag-<u>on</u>

mermaid
la sirena
la see-<u>reh</u>-na

knight
el caballero
el kaba-<u>yair</u>-o

fairy
el hada
el <u>ah</u>-da

witch
la bruja
la <u>broo</u>-ha

prince
el príncipe
el <u>preen</u>-see-peh

unicorn
el unicornio
el oonee-<u>korn</u>-eeo

vampire
el vampiro
el bam-<u>pee</u>-ro

crown
la corona
la ko<u>ro</u>na

34

Let's play make-believe! - ¡Juguemos a personajes!

sword
la espada
la ess-<u>pah</u>-da

helmet
el yelmo
el <u>yell</u>-moh

castle
el castillo
el kas<u>tee</u>-yo

princess
la princesa
la preen-<u>sess</u>a

king
el rey
el ray

queen
la reina
la <u>ray</u>-na

pirate
el pirata
el pee-<u>rah</u>-ta

pirate ship
el barco pirata
el <u>bar</u>-ko pee-<u>rah</u>-ta

treasure
el tesoro
el tess-<u>oh</u>-ro

Transportation - El transporte

el transport-eh

bicycle
la bicicleta
la bee-see-<u>kleh</u>-ta

motorcycle
la motocicleta
la moto-see-<u>kleh</u>-ta

scooter
el scooter
el es-<u>koo</u>-tair

truck
el camión
el kam-<u>yon</u>

van
la furgoneta
la foor-go<u>neh</u>-ta

pickup truck
la camioneta
la kam-yon-<u>eh</u>-ta

scooter
el patinete
el pa-teen-<u>eh</u>-teh

tram
el tranvía
el tran-<u>bee</u>-ya

stroller
el cochecito
el kotch-eh-<u>see</u>-toh

36

Vroom, vroom! - ¡Brrrum, brrrum!

broom broom

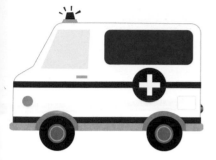

ambulance
la ambulancia
la amboo-<u>lan</u>-see-a

fire engine
el camión de bomberos
el kam-<u>yon</u> deh bom<u>bair</u>-oss

helicopter
el helicóptero
el elee-<u>kop</u>-tairo

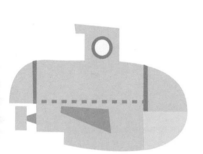

submarine
el submarino
el sub-mar-<u>ee</u>-no

hot air balloon
el globo aerostático
el <u>glo</u>-bo airo-<u>stat</u>-eek-o

quad bike
el cuatriciclo
el kwatree-<u>seek</u>-lo

cruise ship
el crucero
el kroo-<u>sair</u>-o

tractor
el tractor
el trak-<u>tor</u>

taxi
el taxi
el <u>taxee</u>

37

At sea - En el mar
en el mar

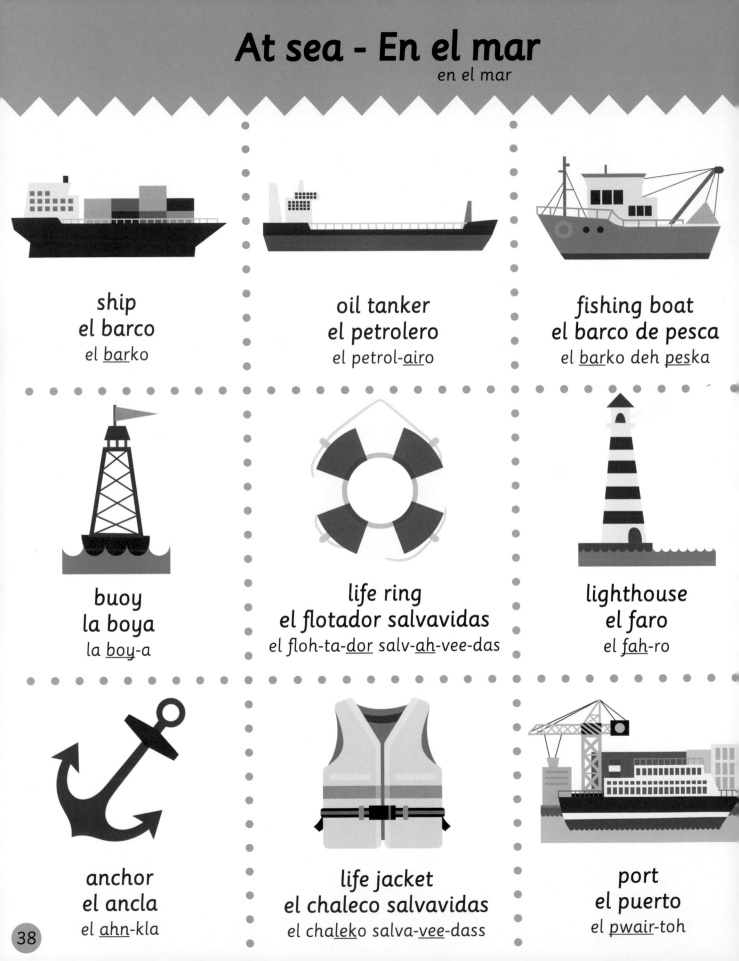

ship
el barco
el <u>bar</u>ko

oil tanker
el petrolero
el petrol-<u>airo</u>

fishing boat
el barco de pesca
el <u>bar</u>ko deh <u>pes</u>ka

buoy
la boya
la <u>boy</u>-a

life ring
el flotador salvavidas
el floh-ta-<u>dor</u> salv-<u>ah</u>-vee-das

lighthouse
el faro
el <u>fah</u>-ro

anchor
el ancla
el <u>ahn</u>-kla

life jacket
el chaleco salvavidas
el cha<u>le</u>ko salva-<u>vee</u>-dass

port
el puerto
el <u>pwair</u>-toh

Apartment building - El edificio de apartamentos

el ed-ee-<u>fee</u>-see-o deh app-ar-ta-<u>men</u>-toss

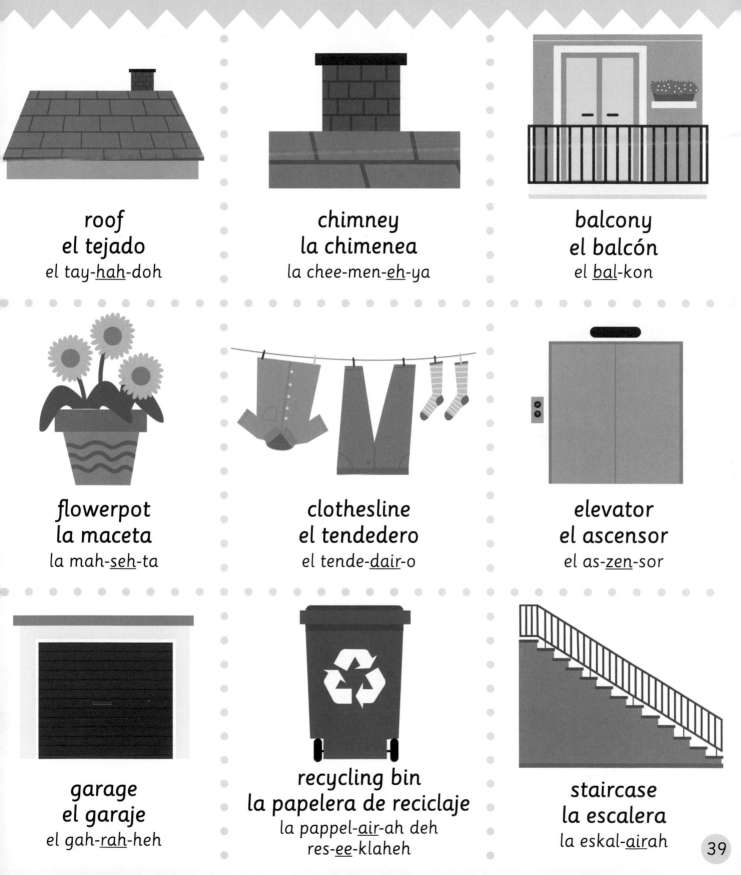

roof
el tejado
el tay-<u>hah</u>-doh

chimney
la chimenea
la chee-men-<u>eh</u>-ya

balcony
el balcón
el <u>bal</u>-kon

flowerpot
la maceta
la mah-<u>seh</u>-ta

clothesline
el tendedero
el tende-<u>dair</u>-o

elevator
el ascensor
el as-<u>zen</u>-sor

garage
el garaje
el gah-<u>rah</u>-heh

recycling bin
la papelera de reciclaje
la pappel-<u>air</u>-ah deh
res-<u>ee</u>-klaheh

staircase
la escalera
la eskal-<u>airah</u>

Building site - La obra
la <u>ob</u>-ra

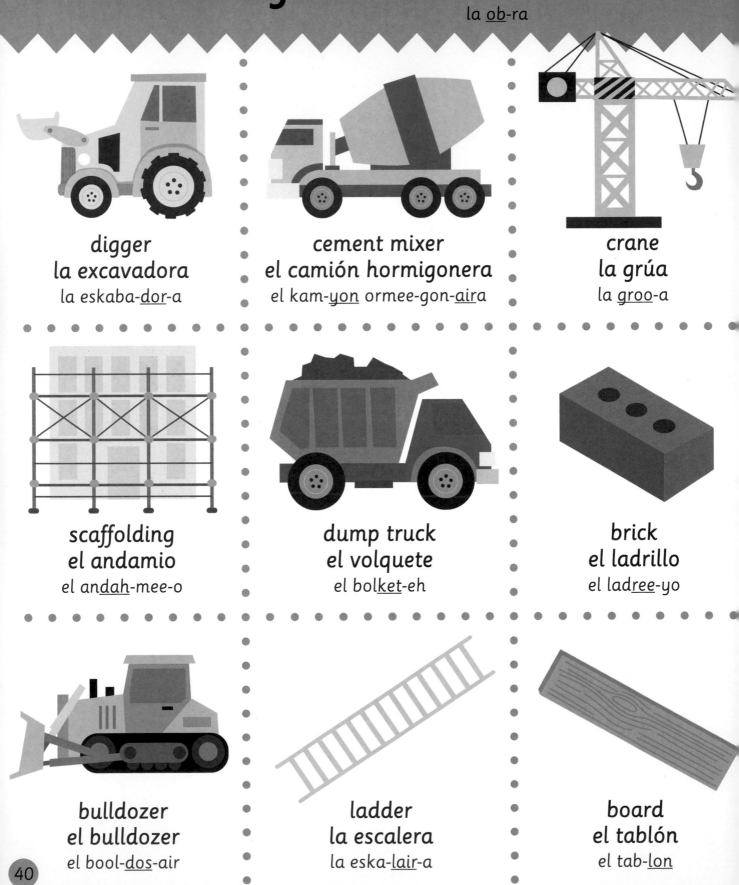

digger
la excavadora
la eskaba-<u>dor</u>-a

cement mixer
el camión hormigonera
el kam-<u>yon</u> ormee-gon-<u>aira</u>

crane
la grúa
la <u>groo</u>-a

scaffolding
el andamio
el a<u>ndah</u>-mee-o

dump truck
el volquete
el bol<u>ket</u>-eh

brick
el ladrillo
el lad<u>ree</u>-yo

bulldozer
el bulldozer
el bool-<u>dos</u>-air

ladder
la escalera
la eska-<u>lair</u>-a

board
el tablón
el tab-<u>lon</u>

40

Tools - Las herramientas
lass errah-<u>meeyen</u>-tass

rake
el rastrillo
el ras<u>tree</u>-yo

wheelbarrow
la carretilla
la kare<u>tee</u>-ya

hammer
el martillo
el mar-<u>tee</u>-yo

nail
el clavo
el <u>klah</u>-bo

saw
el serrucho
el sair-<u>oo</u>cho

hose
la manguera
la man-<u>gair</u>-a

drill
el taladro
el ta-<u>la</u>-dro

toolbox
la caja de herramientas
la <u>ka</u>ha deh errah-<u>meeyen</u>-tass

screwdriver
el destornillador
el destor-neeya-<u>dor</u>

41

Travel - El viaje

el bee-ah-heh

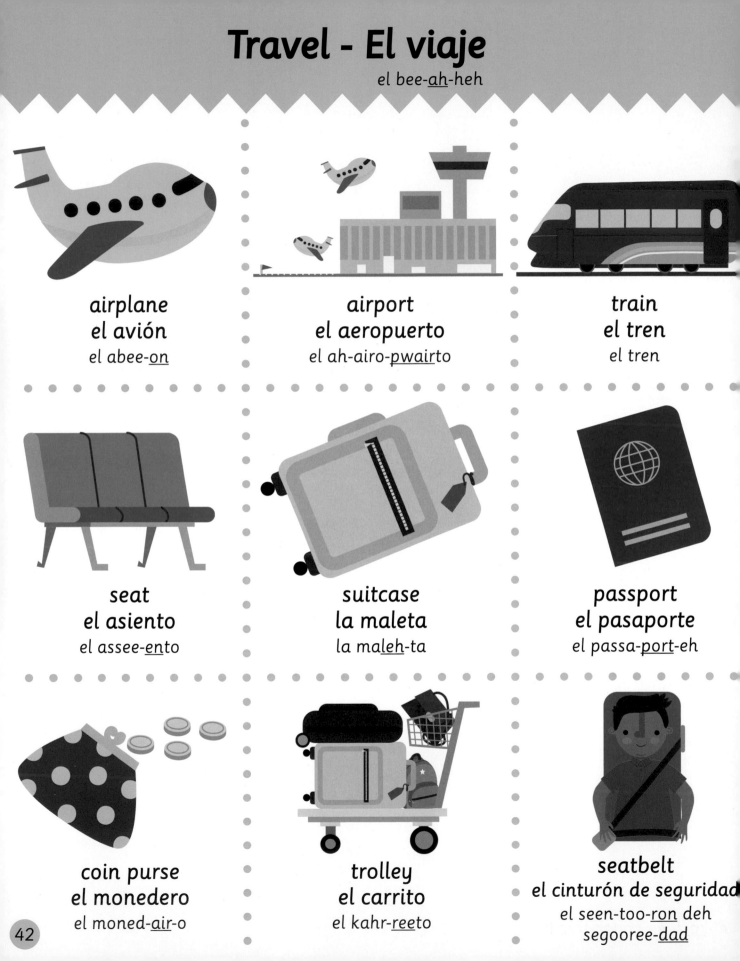

airplane
el avión
el abee-on

airport
el aeropuerto
el ah-airo-pwairto

train
el tren
el tren

seat
el asiento
el assee-ento

suitcase
la maleta
la maleh-ta

passport
el pasaporte
el passa-port-eh

coin purse
el monedero
el moned-air-o

trolley
el carrito
el kahr-reeto

seatbelt
el cinturón de seguridad
el seen-too-ron deh segooree-dad

42

Let's go! - ¡Vámonos!
bah-mo-noss

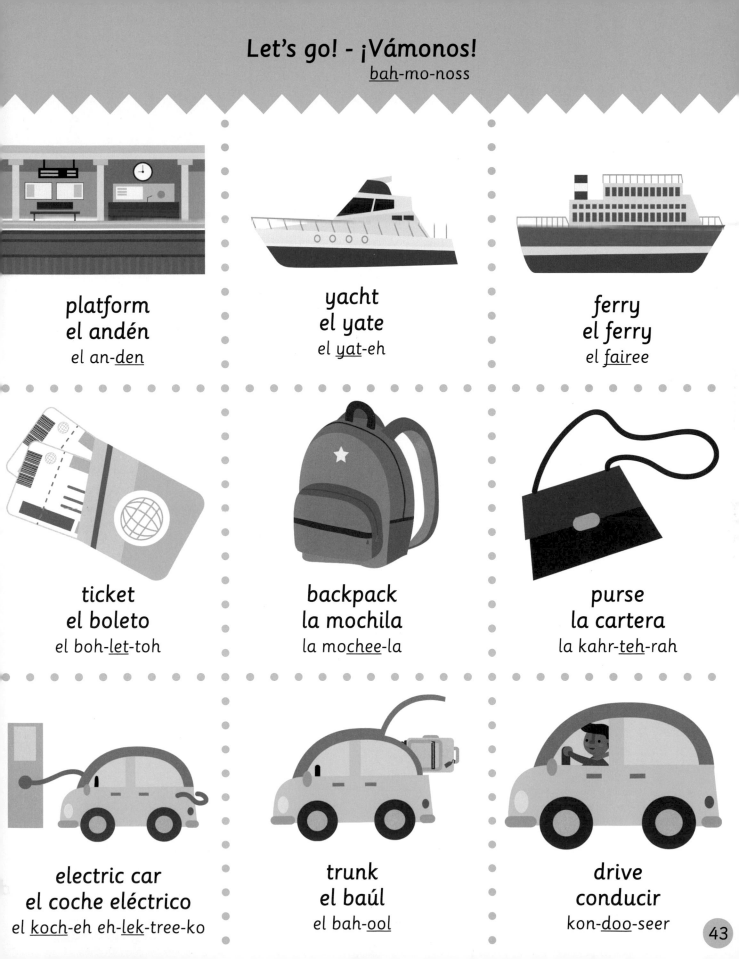

platform
el andén
el an-den

yacht
el yate
el yat-eh

ferry
el ferry
el fairee

ticket
el boleto
el boh-let-toh

backpack
la mochila
la mochee-la

purse
la cartera
la kahr-teh-rah

electric car
el coche eléctrico
el koch-eh eh-lek-tree-ko

trunk
el baúl
el bah-ool

drive
conducir
kon-doo-seer

43

In town - En la ciudad
en la see-oo-<u>dad</u>

house
la casa
la <u>kah</u>-sa

street
la calle
la <u>kah</u>-yeh

sidewalk
la acera
la ah-<u>sair</u>-a

streetlight
la farola
la fah-<u>roh</u>-la

store
la tienda
la tee-<u>en</u>da

bakery
la panadería
la panadair-<u>ee</u>-a

butcher shop
la carnicería
la karneesair-<u>ee</u>-a

café
el café
el caf<u>eh</u>

trash can
el bote de basura
el <u>boh</u>-teh deh ba-<u>soo</u>-ra

Let's look around - Echemos un vistazo
etch-eh-moss oon bees-ta-so

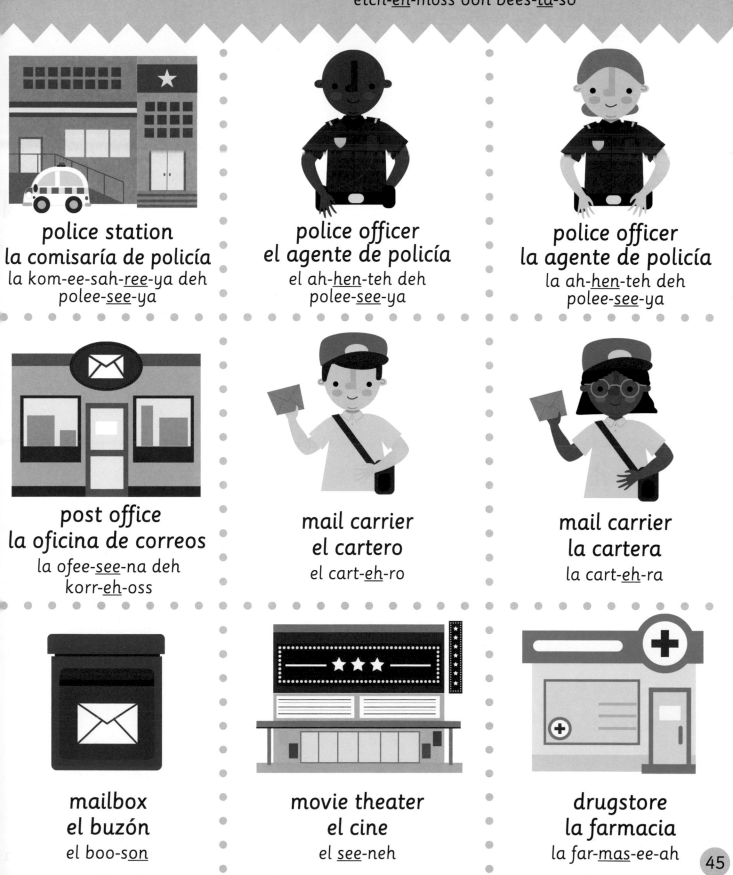

police station
la comisaría de policía
la kom-ee-sah-ree-ya deh polee-see-ya

police officer
el agente de policía
el ah-hen-teh deh polee-see-ya

police officer
la agente de policía
la ah-hen-teh deh polee-see-ya

post office
la oficina de correos
la ofee-see-na deh korr-eh-oss

mail carrier
el cartero
el cart-eh-ro

mail carrier
la cartera
la cart-eh-ra

mailbox
el buzón
el boo-son

movie theater
el cine
el see-neh

drugstore
la farmacia
la far-mas-ee-ah

45

On the road - En la carretera

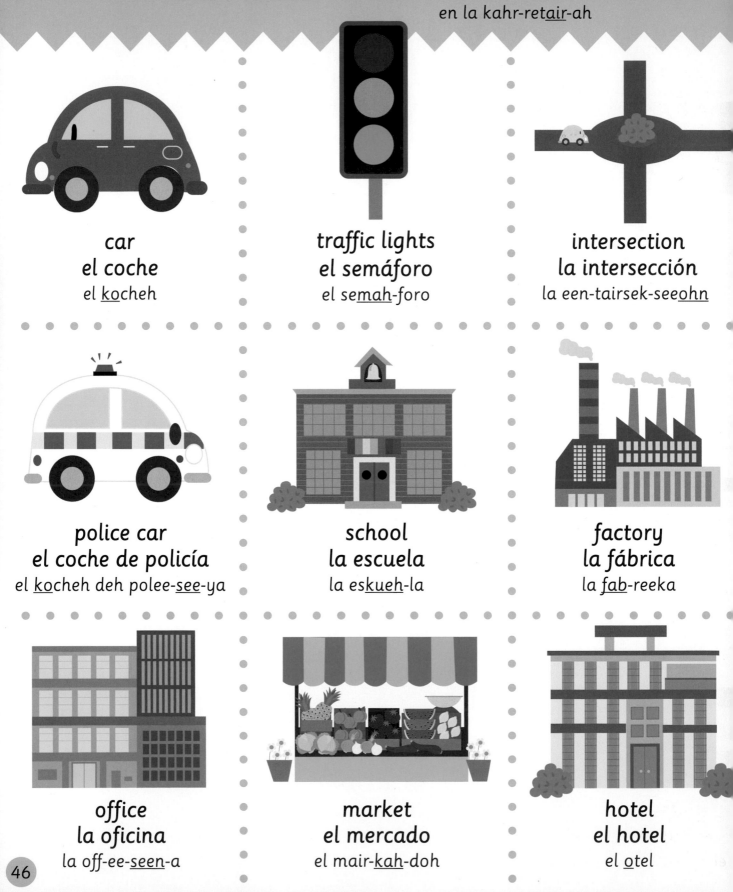

car
el coche
el <u>ko</u>cheh

traffic lights
el semáforo
el s<u>emah</u>-foro

intersection
la intersección
la een-tairsek-see<u>ohn</u>

police car
el coche de policía
el <u>ko</u>cheh deh polee-<u>see</u>-ya

school
la escuela
la es<u>kueh</u>-la

factory
la fábrica
la <u>fab</u>-reeka

office
la oficina
la off-ee-<u>seen</u>-a

market
el mercado
el mair-<u>kah</u>-doh

hotel
el hotel
el <u>o</u>tel

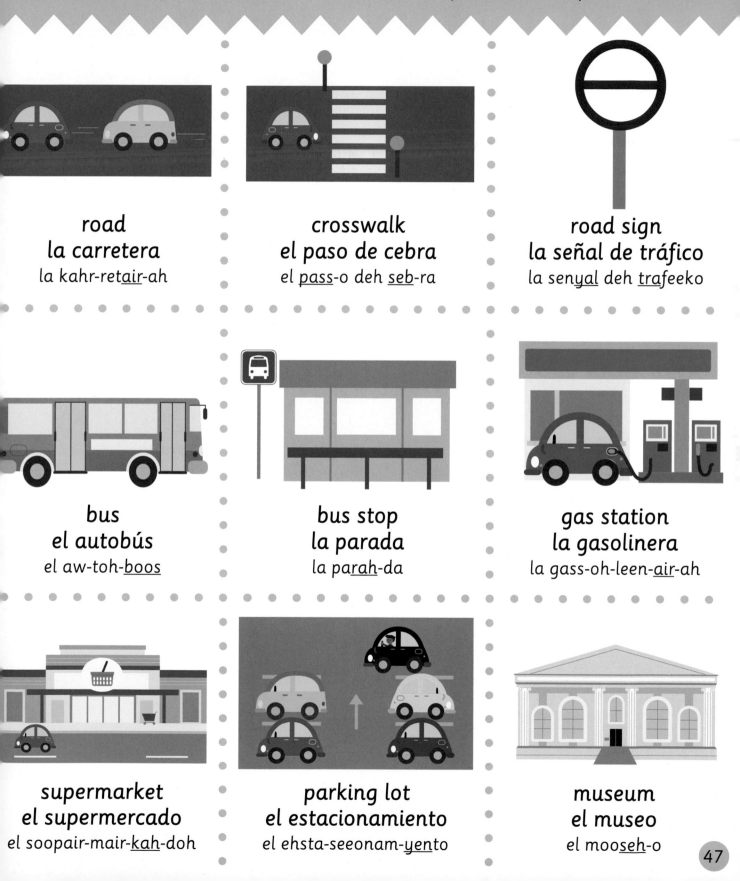

road
la carretera
la kahr-ret<u>air</u>-ah

crosswalk
el paso de cebra
el <u>pass</u>-o deh <u>seb</u>-ra

road sign
la señal de tráfico
la sen<u>yal</u> deh <u>trafeeko</u>

bus
el autobús
el aw-toh-<u>boos</u>

bus stop
la parada
la p<u>arah</u>-da

gas station
la gasolinera
la gass-oh-leen-<u>air</u>-ah

supermarket
el supermercado
el soopair-mair-<u>kah</u>-doh

parking lot
el estacionamiento
el ehsta-seeonam-<u>yen</u>to

museum
el museo
el moo<u>seh</u>-o

47

Supermarket - El supermercado

el soopair-mair-<u>kah</u>-doh

food
la comida
la ko-<u>mee</u>-da

bread
el pan
el pan

meat
la carne
la <u>kar</u>-neh

rice
el arroz
el ahr-<u>rohs</u>

fish
el pescado
el pes<u>kah</u>-doh

butter
la mantequilla
la manteh-<u>kee</u>-ya

pasta
la pasta
la <u>pas</u>-ta

sugar
el azúcar
el ah-<u>soo</u>-kar

shopping cart
el carrito
el kahr-<u>reeto</u>

48

What do you like to eat? - ¿Qué te gusta comer?

keh teh <u>goos</u>-ta koh-<u>mer</u>

egg
el huevo
el <u>weh</u>-bo

cheese
el queso
el <u>keh</u>-so

chicken
el pollo
el <u>po</u>-yo

sausage
la salchicha
la sal<u>chee</u>-cha

milk
la leche
la <u>leh</u>-cheh

yogurt
el yogur
el yog-<u>oor</u>

basket
la cesta
la <u>sess</u>-ta

shopping bag
la bolsa de la compra
la <u>bol</u>sa deh la <u>kom</u>pra

money
el dinero
el dee<u>nair</u>o

Fruit - La fruta
la froo-ta

apple
la manzana
la man-<u>sah</u>-na

peach
el melocotón
el melo-ko-<u>ton</u>

cherries
las cerezas
lass sair-<u>eh</u>-sahss

banana
el plátano
el <u>plah</u>-tan-o

grapes
las uvas
lass <u>oo</u>bass

strawberry
la fresa
la <u>freh</u>-sa

watermelon
la sandía
la san-<u>dee</u>-ya

melon
el melón
el meh-<u>lohn</u>

coconut
el coco
el <u>ko</u>-ko

orange
la naranja
la nah-<u>ran</u>-ha

pineapple
la piña
la <u>peen</u>-ya

mango
el mango
el <u>man</u>go

lemon
el limón
el lee<u>mon</u>

kiwi
el kiwi
el <u>kee</u>-wee

pear
la pera
la <u>pair</u>-a

plum
la ciruela
la see-roo-<u>eh</u>-la

blueberries
los arándanos
loss ah-<u>ran</u>-dan-oss

raspberry
la frambuesa
la fram-<u>bweh</u>-sa

Vegetables - Las verduras

lass bair-doo-rass

potato
la papa
la pah-pah

corn
el maíz
el mah-ees

cabbage
la col
la kol

tomato
el tomate
el tom-ah-teh

lettuce
la lechuga
la let-choo-ga

cucumber
el pepino
el pepeeno

peas
los guisantes
loss gui-sahn-tess

pumpkin
la calabaza
la kala-bas-a

broccoli
el brócoli
el brok-olee

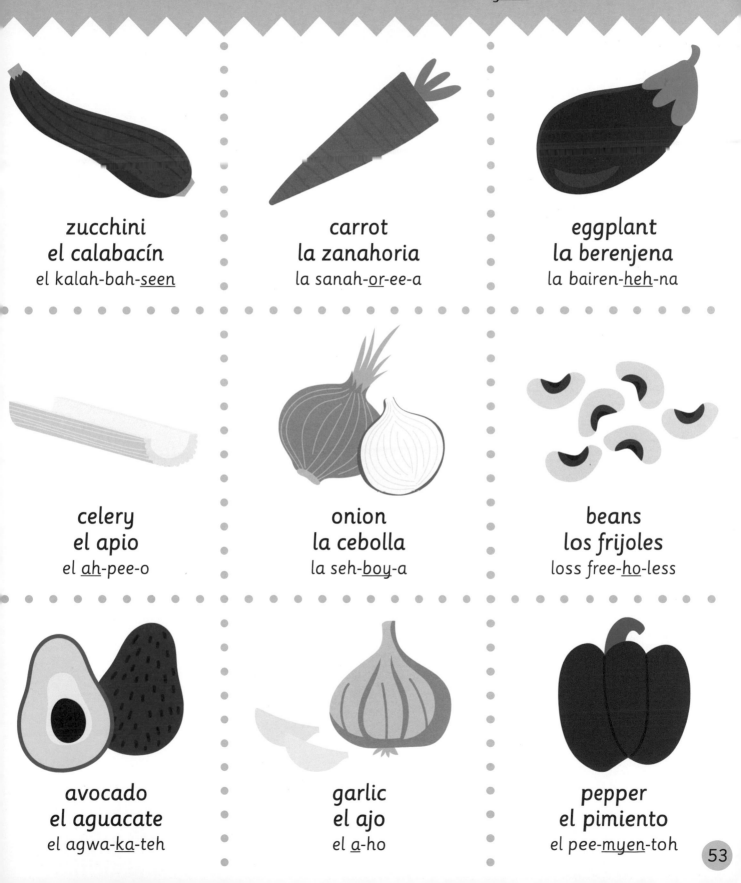

zucchini
el calabacín
el kalah-bah-<u>seen</u>

carrot
la zanahoria
la sanah-<u>or</u>-ee-a

eggplant
la berenjena
la bairen-<u>heh</u>-na

celery
el apio
el <u>ah</u>-pee-o

onion
la cebolla
la seh-<u>boy</u>-a

beans
los frijoles
loss free-<u>ho</u>-less

avocado
el aguacate
el agwa-<u>ka</u>-teh

garlic
el ajo
el <u>a</u>-ho

pepper
el pimiento
el pee-<u>myen</u>-toh

Countryside - El campo
el kampo

woods
el bosque
el boss-keh

field
el prado
el prah-doh

mountain
la montaña
la mon-tan-ya

windmill
el molino
el moh-lee-no

gate
la puerta de la verja
la pwairta deh la bair-ha

wall
el muro
el moo-ro

badger
el tejón
el teh-hon

fox
el zorro
el sor-ro

squirrel
la ardilla
la ardee-ya

Smell the fresh air! - ¡Respira aire fresco!

ress-<u>pee</u>-ra <u>ay</u>-re <u>fress</u>-ko

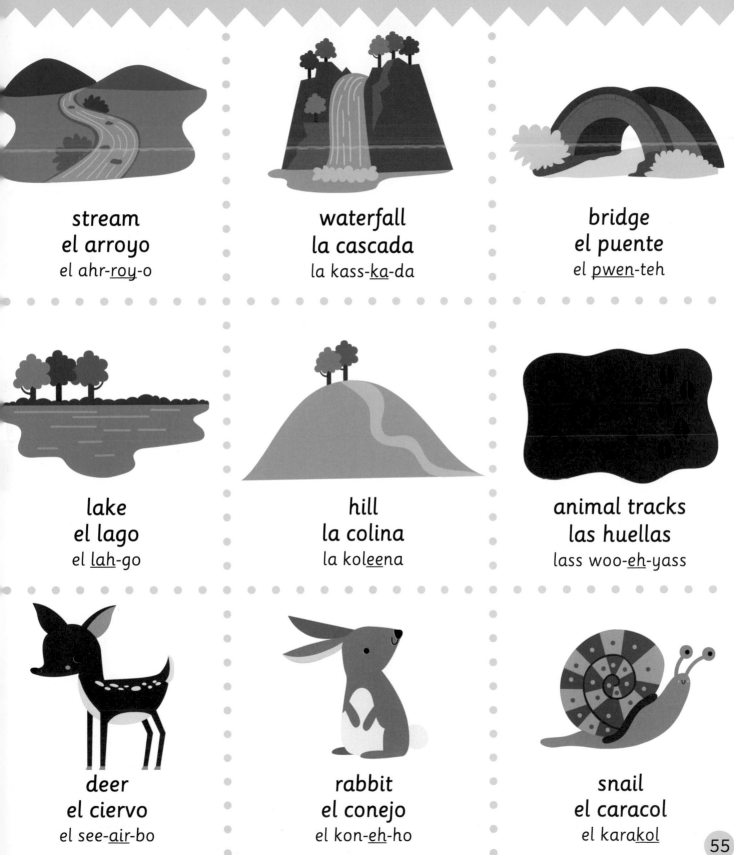

stream
el arroyo
el ahr-<u>roy</u>-o

waterfall
la cascada
la kass-<u>ka</u>-da

bridge
el puente
el <u>pwen</u>-teh

lake
el lago
el <u>lah</u>-go

hill
la colina
la kol<u>ee</u>na

animal tracks
las huellas
lass woo-<u>eh</u>-yass

deer
el ciervo
el see-<u>air</u>-bo

rabbit
el conejo
el kon-<u>eh</u>-ho

snail
el caracol
el kara<u>kol</u>

Forest - El bosque

el <u>boss</u>-keh

pine tree
el pino
el <u>peen</u>-oh

trunk
el tronco
el <u>tron</u>-ko

branch
la rama
la <u>ra</u>-ma

stick
el palo
el <u>pah</u>-lo

leaf
la hoja
la <u>o</u>-ha

pine cone
la piña
la <u>peen</u>-ya

log
el tronco
el <u>tron</u>-ko

petal
el pétalo
el <u>peh</u>-ta-lo

root
la raíz
la ra-<u>ees</u>

56

Insects - Los insectos
loss een-<u>sek</u>-toss

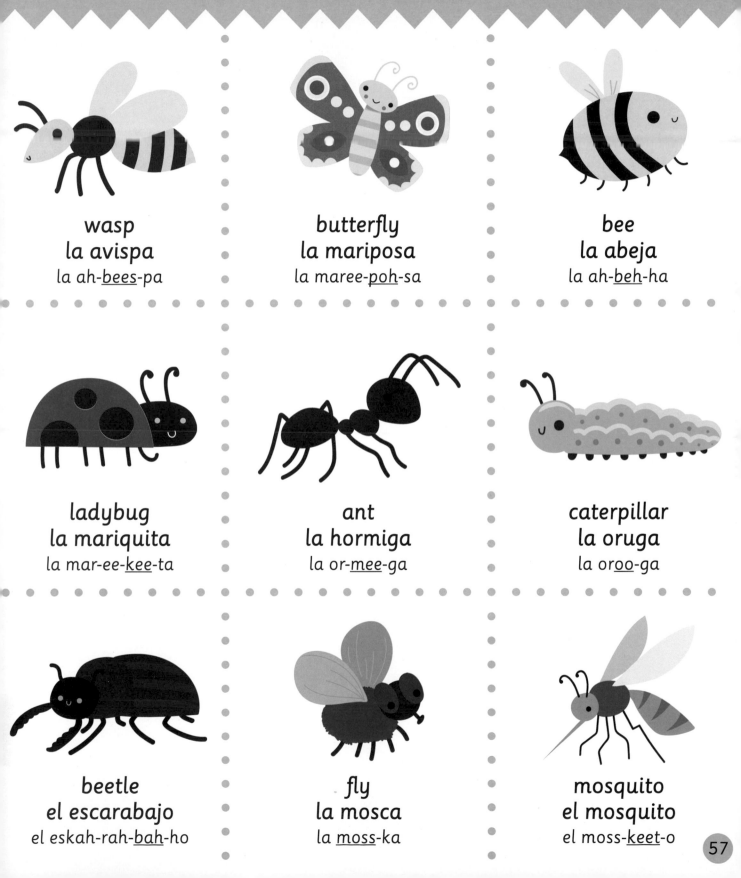

wasp
la avispa
la ah-<u>bees</u>-pa

butterfly
la mariposa
la maree-<u>poh</u>-sa

bee
la abeja
la ah-<u>beh</u>-ha

ladybug
la mariquita
la mar-ee-<u>kee</u>-ta

ant
la hormiga
la or-<u>mee</u>-ga

caterpillar
la oruga
la or<u>oo</u>-ga

beetle
el escarabajo
el eskah-rah-<u>bah</u>-ho

fly
la mosca
la <u>moss</u>-ka

mosquito
el mosquito
el moss-<u>keet</u>-o

57

Weather - El tiempo
el tee-empo

sunshine
el sol
el sol

it is hot
hace calor
ah-seh ka-lor

sunglasses
las gafas de sol
lass gaf-ass deh sol

clouds
las nubes
lass noo-bess

wind
el viento
el bee-en-toh

fog
la niebla
la nee-ehbla

snow
la nieve
la nee-eh-beh

it is cold
hace frío
ah-seh freeo

gloves
los guantes
loss gwan-tess

What a beautiful day! - ¡Qué día tan bonito!

keh <u>dee</u>-a tan bo-<u>nee</u>-toh

rain
la lluvia
la <u>yoo</u>-beea

umbrella
el paraguas
el par-<u>ag</u>-wass

puddle
el charco
el <u>char</u>-ko

lightning
el relámpago
el rel-l<u>am</u>-pago

thunder
el trueno
el troo<u>weh</u>-no

storm
la tormenta
la tor-<u>men</u>-ta

ice
el hielo
el <u>yeh</u>-lo

snowman
el muñeco de nieve
el moon-<u>yek</u>-o deh nee-<u>eh</u>-beh

rainbow
el arco iris
el <u>ar</u>ko <u>eer</u>-iss

59

Beach - La playa
la pl<u>ah</u>-ya

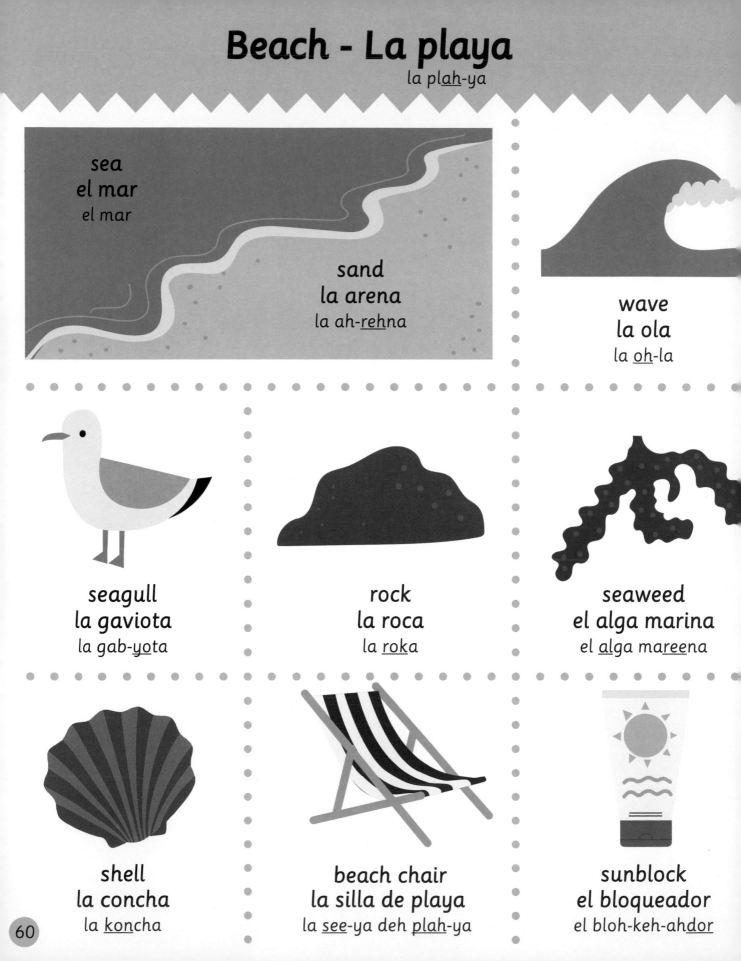

sea
el mar
el mar

sand
la arena
la ah-<u>reh</u>na

wave
la ola
la <u>oh</u>-la

seagull
la gaviota
la gab-<u>yo</u>ta

rock
la roca
la <u>ro</u>ka

seaweed
el alga marina
el <u>al</u>ga ma<u>ree</u>na

shell
la concha
la <u>kon</u>cha

beach chair
la silla de playa
la <u>see</u>-ya deh <u>plah</u>-ya

sunblock
el bloqueador
el bloh-keh-ah<u>dor</u>

What can you see? - ¿Qué ves?

beach umbrella
la sombrilla
la som*bree*-ya

pail
el cubo
el *koo*-bo

shovel
la pala
la *pah*-la

sun hat
el sombrero
el som-*brair*-o

swim ring
el flotador
el floh-ta-*dor*

sandcastle
el castillo de arena
el kas*tee*-yo deh ah-*reh*na

surfboard
la tabla de surf
la *tah*-bla deh soorf

surfer
el / la surfista
el/la soor-*fee*sta

sailboat
el velero
el be*lair*-o

61

Under the sea - El fondo del mar

el <u>fon</u>do del mar

dolphin
el delfín
el del-<u>feen</u>

crab
el crangrejo
el kan<u>greh</u>-ho

turtle
la tortuga
la tor-<u>tooga</u>

octopus
el pulpo
el <u>pool</u>-po

shark
el tiburón
el teeboo-<u>ron</u>

whale
la ballena
la ba-<u>yeh</u>-na

jellyfish
la medusa
la me<u>doo</u>-sa

starfish
la estrella de mar
la ess<u>treh</u>-ya deh mar

scuba diving
el buceo
el boo-<u>seh</u>-o

62

Space - El espacio

el espas-eeo

Earth
la Tierra
la teeair-rah

sky
el cielo
el see-ehlo

Sun
el sol
el sol

Moon
la luna
la loona

star
la estrella
la esstreh-ya

rocket
el cohete
el ko-eh-teh

planet
el planeta
el pla-neh-ta

astronaut
el / la astronauta
el/la astrona-oo-ta

satellite
el satélite
el satel-eeteh

63

At school - En la escuela

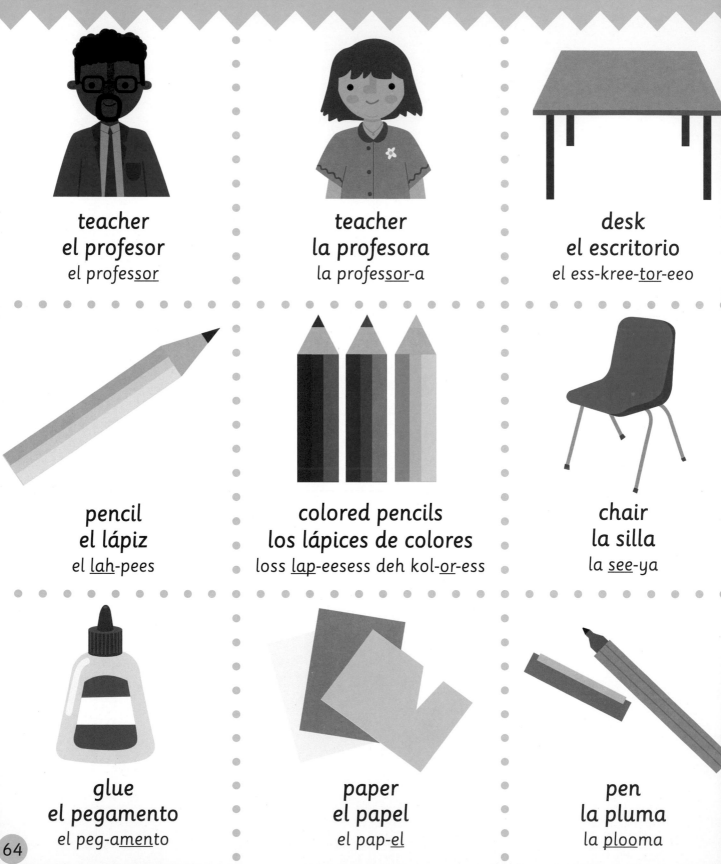

teacher
el profesor
el profes<u>sor</u>

teacher
la profesora
la profes<u>sor</u>-a

desk
el escritorio
el ess-kree-<u>tor</u>-eeo

pencil
el lápiz
el <u>lah</u>-pees

colored pencils
los lápices de colores
loss <u>lap</u>-eesess deh kol-<u>or</u>-ess

chair
la silla
la <u>see</u>-ya

glue
el pegamento
el peg-<u>amen</u>to

paper
el papel
el pap-<u>el</u>

pen
la pluma
la <u>ploo</u>ma

64

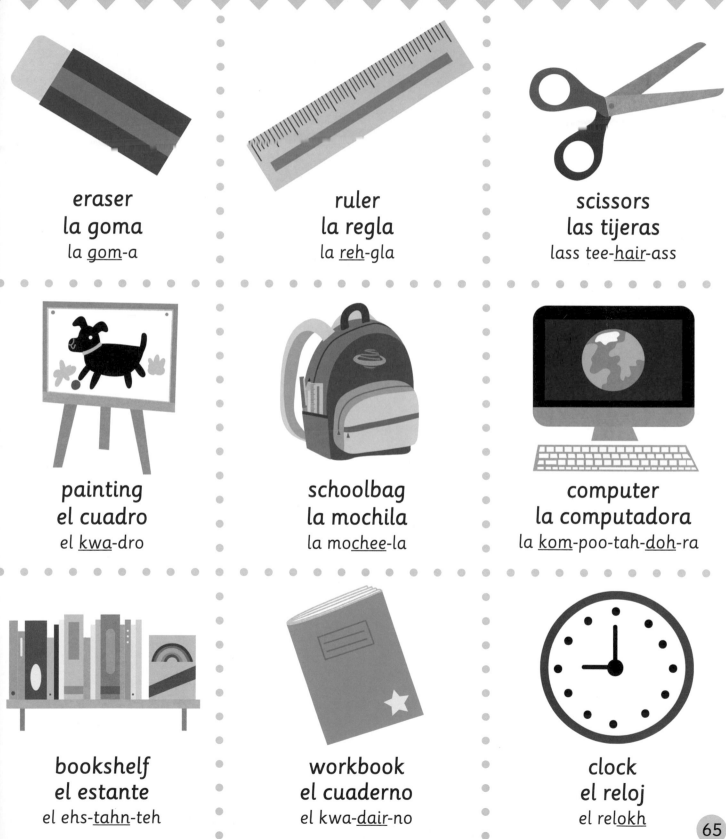

eraser
la goma
la <u>gom</u>-a

ruler
la regla
la <u>reh</u>-gla

scissors
las tijeras
lass tee-<u>hair</u>-ass

painting
el cuadro
el <u>kwa</u>-dro

schoolbag
la mochila
la mo<u>chee</u>-la

computer
la computadora
la <u>kom</u>-poo-tah-<u>doh</u>-ra

bookshelf
el estante
el ehs-<u>tahn</u>-teh

workbook
el cuaderno
el kwa-<u>dair</u>-no

clock
el reloj
el re<u>lokh</u>

Sports - Los deportes

loss dep-<u>or</u>tess

soccer
el fútbol
el <u>foot</u>-bol

running
correr
kohr-<u>rair</u>

cycling
ir en bicicleta
eer en bee-see-<u>klet</u>-a

skiing
esquiar
ess-kee-<u>ar</u>

gymnastics
la gimnasia
la him-<u>nass</u>-eea

swimming
nadar
nah-<u>dar</u>

athletics
el atletismo
el atlet-<u>eess</u>mo

tennis
el tenis
el ten-<u>eess</u>

basketball
el baloncesto
el balon-<u>sess</u>-sto

66

I enjoy... - Me gusta...
meh goos-ta

riding
la equitación
la ekee-tasee-yon

diving
zambullirme
zam-boo-yeer-meh

climbing
escalar
eskal-ar

walking
andar
andar

sailing
la navegación
la nabeh-gasee-yon

fishing
pescar
pess-kar

yoga
el yoga
el yoga

doing a cartwheel
hacer una voltereta
asair oona vol-teh-reh-ta

doing a handstand
pararse de manos
pah-rahr-seh deh
mah-noss

67

Action words - Las acciones

crawling
gatear
gateh-ar

carrying
cargar
kargar

kissing
besar
besar

hugging
abrazar
abra-sar

standing
estar de pie
estar deh pee-eh

sitting
estar sentado
estar sentah-doh

pulling
estirar
esstee-rar

pushing
empujar
empoo-har

playing
jugar
hoo-gar

singing
cantar
kant<u>ar</u>

reading
leer
leh-<u>air</u>

writing
escribir
esskr<u>ee</u>-b<u>eer</u>

drawing
dibujar
deeboo-<u>har</u>

eating
comer
kom<u>air</u>

drinking
beber
beh-<u>bair</u>

washing
lavarse
la-<u>bar</u>-seh

brushing my teeth
lavarme los dientes
la-<u>bar</u>-meh loss dee-<u>yen</u>-tess

going to bed
irme a la cama
<u>eer</u>-meh ah la <u>kah</u>-ma

Using adjectives - Los adjetivos

Adjectives change depending on the gender of the noun that they are describing. Remember that the gender of a noun is about grammar and not necessarily about the gender of the animal or person. The easiest rule to memorize is that adjectives describing masculine nouns end in "o" and those describing feminine nouns end in "a." If the adjective ends in "e" or "z," it does not change.

**the elephant is big
el elefante es grande**
el eleh-<u>fan</u>-teh ess <u>gran</u>-deh

**the whale is big
la ballena es grande**
la ba-<u>yeh</u>-na ess <u>gran</u>-deh

**the rabbit is small
el conejo es pequeño**
el kon-<u>eh</u>-ho ess pek<u>en</u>-yo

**the fly is small
la mosca es pequeña**
la <u>moss</u>-ka ess pek<u>en</u>-ya

**the boy is happy
el niño es feliz**
el n<u>een</u>-yo ess fel-<u>ees</u>

**the girl is happy
la niña es feliz**
la n<u>een</u>-ya ess fel-<u>ees</u>

**the boy is angry
el niño está enfadado**
el n<u>een</u>-yo ess-<u>ta</u> enfad<u>ah</u>-doh

**the girl is angry
la niña está enfadada**
la n<u>een</u>-ya ess-<u>ta</u> enfad<u>ah</u>-da

I am... - Yo soy... / Yo estoy...

yoh soy / yoh ess-<u>toy</u>

Use "**yo soy**" to talk about things that do not change or things that describe your personality, such as being kind or friendly.

Use "**yo estoy**" to talk about things that can change, such as being angry or excited.

kind
atento/atenta
at-<u>en</u>-toh/at-<u>en</u>-ta

friendly
amable
a<u>mah</u>-bleh

angry
enfadado/enfadada
enfad<u>ah</u>-doh/enfad<u>ah</u>-da

happy
feliz
fel-<u>ees</u>

sad
triste
<u>treess</u>-teh

nervous
nervioso/nerviosa
nervee-<u>oss</u>oh/nervee-<u>oss</u>a

confident
confiado/confiada
conf-ee-<u>ah</u>-doh/conf-ee-<u>ah</u>-da

excited
emocionado/emocionada
eh-mos-yo-<u>nad</u>-oh/
eh-mos-yo-<u>nad</u>-a

71

Opposites - Los contrarios

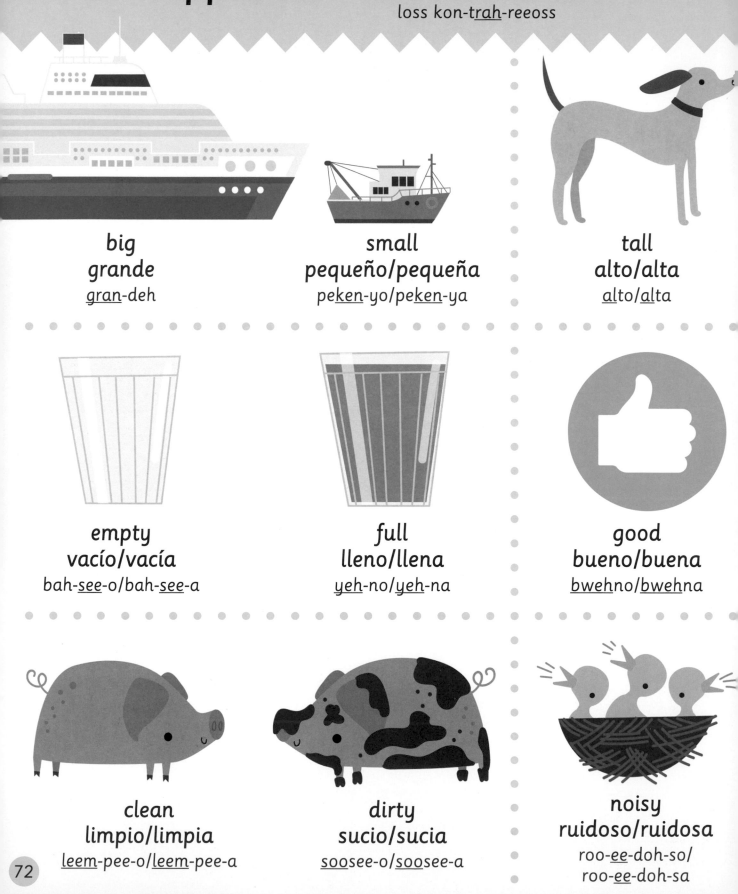

big
grande
gran-deh

small
pequeño/pequeña
pe_ken_-yo/pe_ken_-ya

tall
alto/alta
_al_to/_al_ta

empty
vacío/vacía
bah-_see_-o/bah-_see_-a

full
lleno/llena
yeh-no/_yeh_-na

good
bueno/buena
_bweh_no/_bweh_na

clean
limpio/limpia
leem-pee-o/_leem_-pee-a

dirty
sucio/sucia
_soo_see-o/_soo_see-a

noisy
ruidoso/ruidosa
roo-_ee_-doh-so/
roo-_ee_-doh-sa

72

Who is...? - ¿Quién es...?

short
bajito/bajita
ba-heeto/ba-heeta

light
ligero/ligera
lee-hairo/lee-haira

dark
oscuro/oscura
oss-kooro/oss-koora

bad
malo/mala
mah-lo/mah-la

fast
rápido/rápida
rah-peedo/rah-peeda

slow
lento/lenta
lento/lenta

quiet
tranquilo/tranquila
tran-kee-lo/tran-kee-la

strong
fuerte
fwair-teh

weak
débil
deh-beel

73

Where am I? - ¿Dónde estoy?

don-deh ess-toy

on
sobre
sobreh

under
bajo
bah-ho

inside
dentro
den-tro

outside
fuera
fwe-ra

in front of
delante de
del-an-teh deh

behind
detrás
det-rass

up
arriba
ar-ee-ba

down
abajo
ab-ah-ho

near
cerca
ser-ka

far
lejos
leh-hoss

74

Questions - Preguntas

who?
¿quién?
kyen

what?
¿qué?
keh

when?
¿cuándo?
kwan-doh

where?
¿dónde?
don-deh

why?
¿por qué?
por-keh

how?
¿cómo?
kom-o

how much?
¿cuánto?
kwan-toh

how many?
¿cuántos?
kwan-toss

can I?
¿puedo?
pweh-doh

Seasons and months - Las estaciones y los meses

lass esta-see-<u>on</u>ess ee loss <u>mess</u>ess

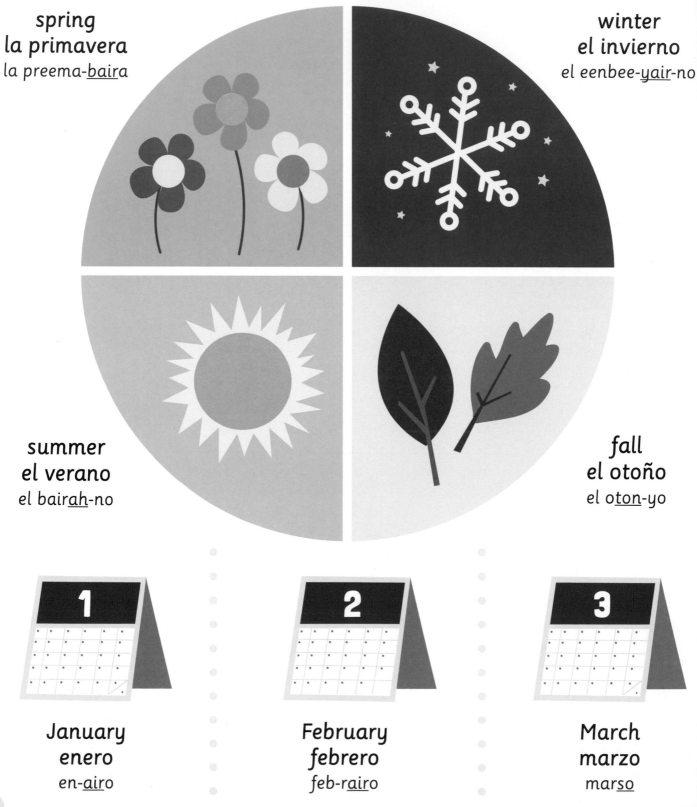

spring
la primavera
la preema-<u>baira</u>

winter
el invierno
el eenbee-<u>yair</u>-no

summer
el verano
el bair<u>ah</u>-no

fall
el otoño
el o<u>ton</u>-yo

1

January
enero
en-<u>airo</u>

2

February
febrero
feb-r<u>airo</u>

3

March
marzo
mar<u>so</u>

When is it hot? - ¿Cuándo hace calor?
kwan-doh _ah_-seh ka-_lor_

April
abril
_ab__reel___

May
mayo
mah-yo

June
junio
hoon-yo

July
julio
hool-yo

August
agosto
ah-_goss_-toh

September
septiembre
sept-_yem_-breh

October
octubre
ok-_too_breh

November
noviembre
nob-_yem_-breh

December
diciembre
deeth-_yem_-breh

Days of the week - Los días de la semana

loss <u>dee</u>-ass deh la sem-<u>ah</u>-na

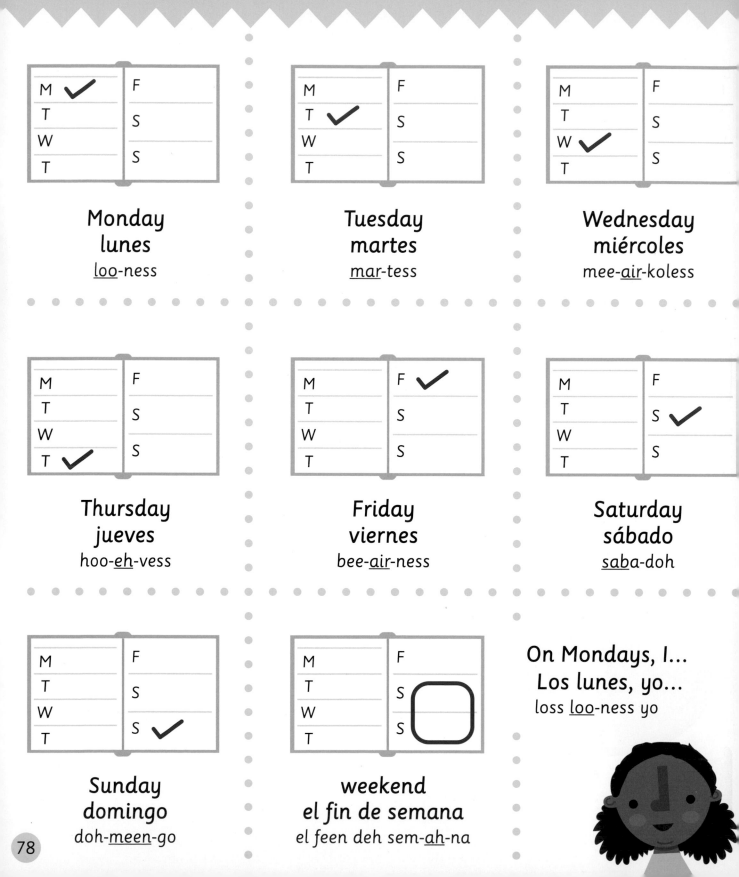

Monday
lunes
<u>loo</u>-ness

Tuesday
martes
<u>mar</u>-tess

Wednesday
miércoles
mee-<u>air</u>-koless

Thursday
jueves
hoo-<u>eh</u>-vess

Friday
viernes
bee-<u>air</u>-ness

Saturday
sábado
<u>saba</u>-doh

Sunday
domingo
doh-<u>meen</u>-go

weekend
el fin de semana
el feen deh sem-<u>ah</u>-na

On Mondays, I...
Los lunes, yo...
loss <u>loo</u>-ness yo

Useful words - Palabras útiles
pa-<u>lab</u>-rass <u>oot</u>-ee-less

today
hoy
oy

yesterday
ayer
ah-ee-<u>air</u>

tomorrow
mañana
man-<u>yah</u>-na

morning
la mañana
la man-<u>yah</u>-na

afternoon
la tarde
la <u>tar</u>-deh

evening
la tarde
la <u>tar</u>-deh

day
el día
el <u>dee</u>-a

right
la derecha
la der-<u>eh</u>-cha

yes
sí
see

night
la noche
la <u>noch</u>-eh

left
la izquierda
la eez-k<u>ier</u>-da

no
no
noh

79

Colors - Los colores
loss kol-_or_-ess

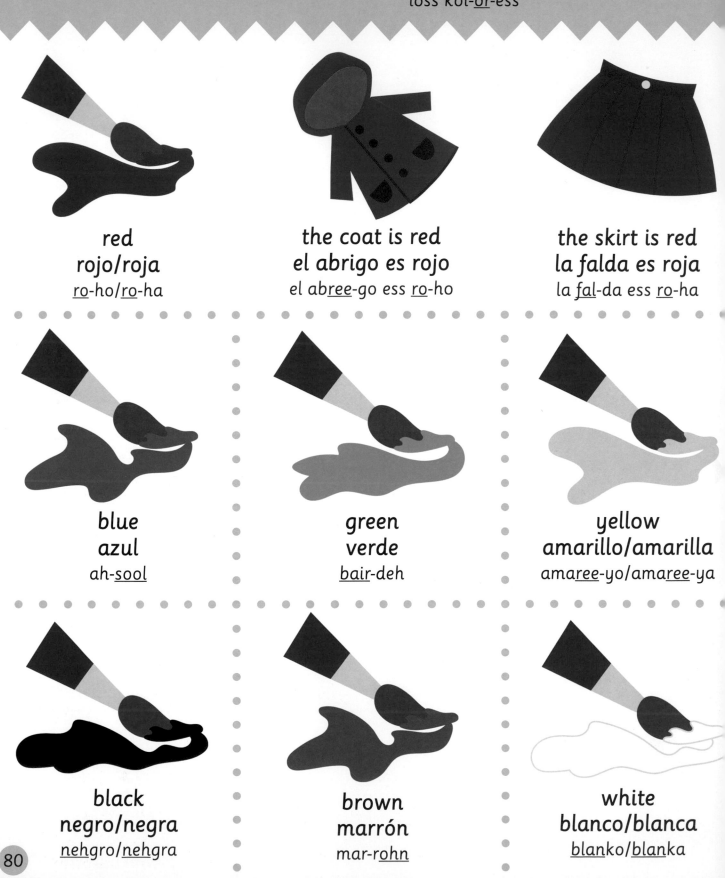

red
rojo/roja
_ro_-ho/_ro_-ha

the coat is red
el abrigo es rojo
el ab_ree_-go ess _ro_-ho

the skirt is red
la falda es roja
la _fal_-da ess _ro_-ha

blue
azul
ah-_sool_

green
verde
bair-deh

yellow
amarillo/amarilla
ama_ree_-yo/ama_ree_-ya

black
negro/negra
_neh_gro/_neh_gra

brown
marrón
mar-_rohn_

white
blanco/blanca
_blan_ko/_blan_ka

What's your favorite color? - ¿Cuál es tu color favorito?

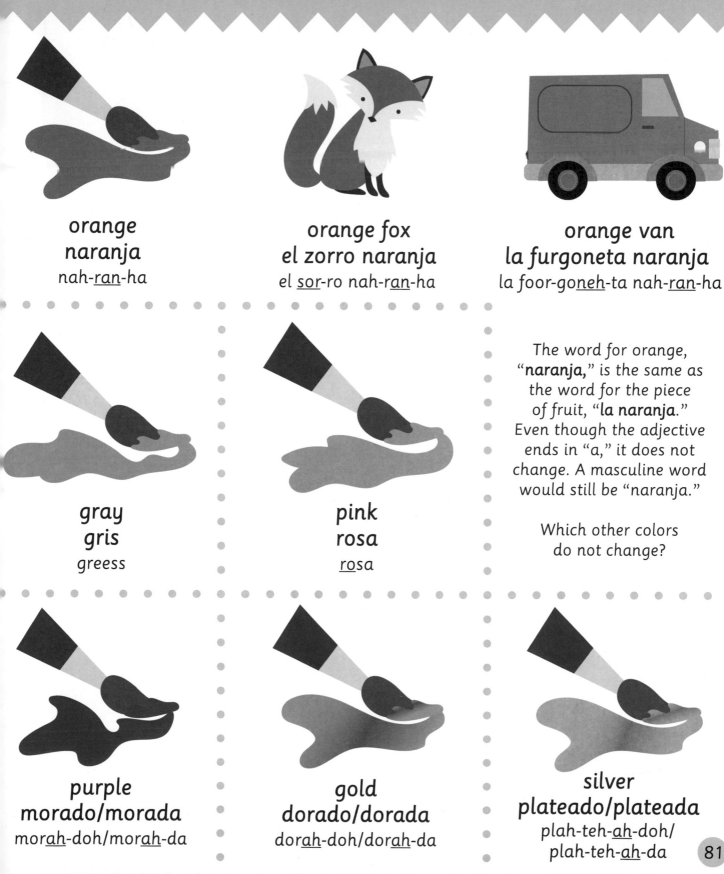

orange
naranja
nah-ran-ha

orange fox
el zorro naranja
el sor-ro nah-ran-ha

orange van
la furgoneta naranja
la foor-goneh-ta nah-ran-ha

gray
gris
greess

pink
rosa
rosa

The word for orange, "**naranja,**" is the same as the word for the piece of fruit, "**la naranja.**" Even though the adjective ends in "a," it does not change. A masculine word would still be "naranja."

Which other colors do not change?

purple
morado/morada
morah-doh/morah-da

gold
dorado/dorada
dorah-doh/dorah-da

silver
plateado/plateada
plah-teh-ah-doh/
plah-teh-ah-da

81

Numbers - Los números

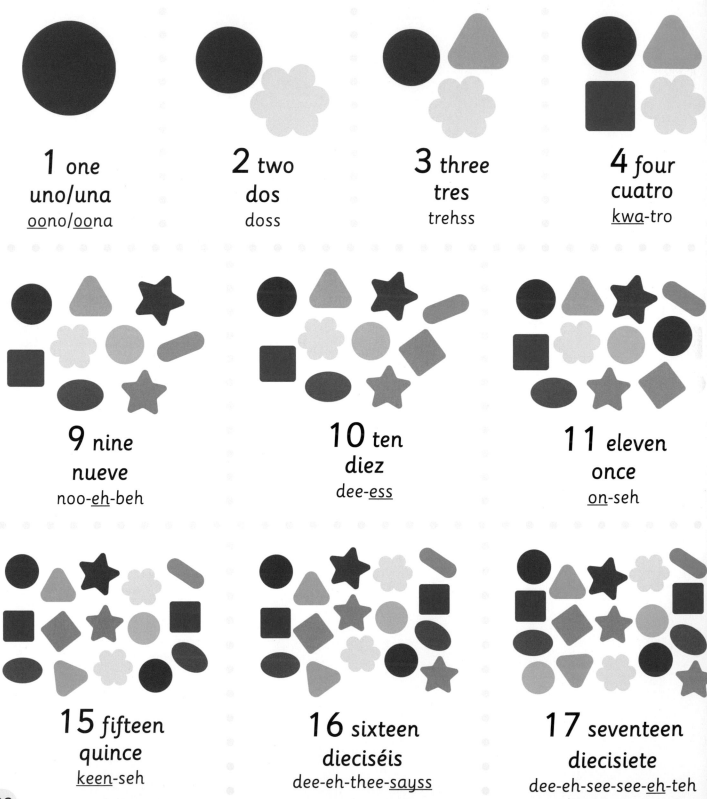

1 one
uno/una
<u>oo</u>no/<u>oo</u>na

2 two
dos
doss

3 three
tres
trehss

4 four
cuatro
<u>kwa</u>-tro

9 nine
nueve
noo-<u>eh</u>-beh

10 ten
diez
dee-<u>ess</u>

11 eleven
once
<u>on</u>-seh

15 fifteen
quince
<u>keen</u>-seh

16 sixteen
dieciséis
dee-eh-thee-<u>sayss</u>

17 seventeen
diecisiete
dee-eh-see-see-<u>eh</u>-teh

Let's count together! - ¡Contemos juntos!

kon-<u>teh</u>-moss <u>hoon</u>-toss

5 *five*
cinco
<u>seen</u>-ko

6 *six*
seis
sayss

7 *seven*
siete
see-<u>eh</u>-teh

8 *eight*
ocho
<u>och</u>-o

12 *twelve*
doce
<u>dos</u>-eh

13 *thirteen*
trece
<u>tres</u>-eh

14 *fourteen*
catorce
kah-<u>tor</u>-seh

18 *eighteen*
dieciocho
dee-eh-see-<u>och</u>-o

19 *nineteen*
diecinueve
dee-eh-see-noo-<u>eh</u>-beh

20 *twenty*
veinte
<u>vayn</u>-teh

Big numbers - Los números altos

loss <u>noo</u>-meh-ross al-<u>toss</u>

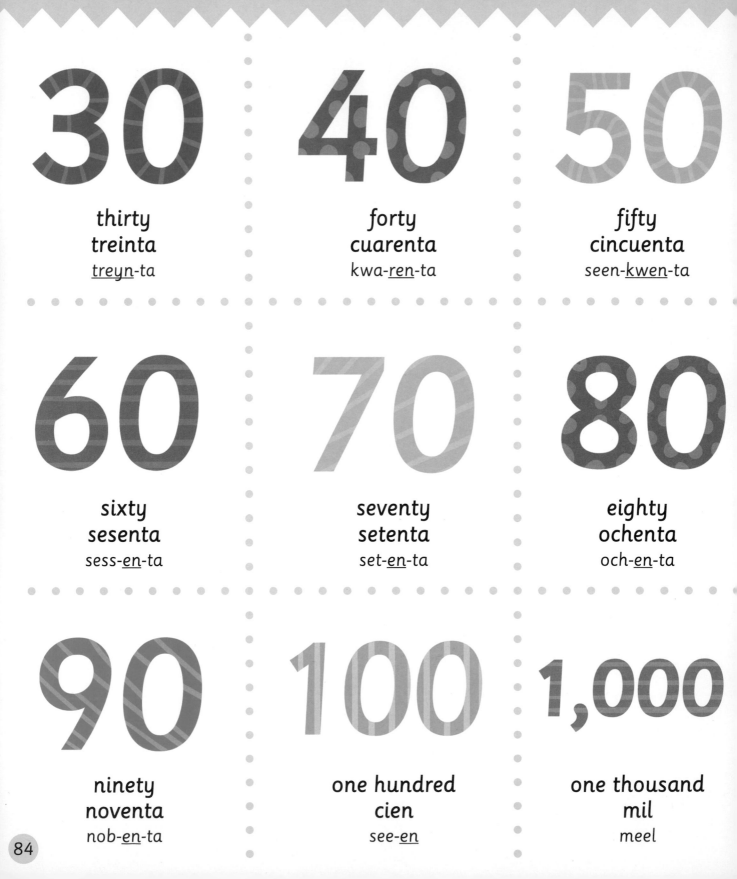

30
thirty
treinta
<u>treyn</u>-ta

40
forty
cuarenta
kwa-<u>ren</u>-ta

50
fifty
cincuenta
seen-<u>kwen</u>-ta

60
sixty
sesenta
sess-<u>en</u>-ta

70
seventy
setenta
set-<u>en</u>-ta

80
eighty
ochenta
och-<u>en</u>-ta

90
ninety
noventa
nob-<u>en</u>-ta

100
one hundred
cien
see-<u>en</u>

1,000
one thousand
mil
meel

The most important words - Las palabras más importantes

lass pa-<u>lab</u>-rass mass eem-por-<u>tan</u>-tess

please
por favor
pohr fab-<u>or</u>

thank you
gracias
<u>gras</u>-ee-ass

Word list - Lista de palabras

<u>leess</u>-ta deh pa-<u>lab</u>-rass

Español/Spanish–Inglés/English

abajo down
la abeja bee
abrazar hugging
el abrigo coat
abril April
la abuela grandmother
el abuelo grandfather
la acera sidewalk
adiós goodbye
el aeropuerto airport
el agente de policía police officer (m)
la agente de policía police officer (f)
agosto August
el agua water
el aguacate avocado
el águila eagle
el ajo garlic
la alfombra rug
el alga marina seaweed
la almohada pillow
alto/alta tall
amable friendly

amarillo/amarilla yellow
la ambulancia ambulance
el ancla anchor
el andamio scaffolding
andar walking
el andén platform
los animales animals
el ansarino gosling
el apio celery
los arándanos blueberries
el árbol tree
el arbusto bush
el arco iris rainbow
la ardilla squirrel
la arena sand
el armario armoire
arriba up
el arroyo stream
el arroz rice
el ascensor elevator
el asiento seat
el astronauta astronaut (m)
la astronauta astronaut (f)
atento/atenta kind

el atletismo athletics
el autobús bus
el avestruz ostrich
el avión airplane
la avispa wasp
ayer yesterday
el azúcar sugar
azul blue
bajito/bajita short
bajo under
el balcón balcony
la ballena whale
el baloncesto basketball
el banco bench
la bañera bathtub
el barco ship
el barco de pesca fishing boat
el barco pirata pirate ship
la barriga stomach
el batido milkshake
el baúl trunk (of car)
beber drinking
la berenjena eggplant
besar kissing

la bicicleta bicycle
blanco/blanca white
el bloqueador sunblock
los bloques blocks
la boca mouth
el boleto ticket
la bolsa de la compra shopping bag
el bosque forest/woods
las botas boots
el bote de basura trash can
el bote de remos rowboat
el botón de oro buttercup
la boya buoy
el brazo arm
el brócoli broccoli
la bruja witch
la brújula compass
el buceo scuba diving
bueno/buena good
buenos días hello
el búho owl
el bulldozer bulldozer
las burbujas bubbles
el burro donkey
el buzón mailbox
el caballero knight
el caballo horse
la cabeza head
la cabra goat
la cacerola saucepan
el cachorro puppy
el café café
la cafetería snack bar
la caja de herramientas toolbox
el cajón drawer
el cajón de arena sandbox
el calabacín zucchini
la calabaza pumpkin
los calcetines socks
la calle street
la cama bed
el camaleón chameleon
el camino path
el camino de piedras stepping stones
el camión truck
el camión de bomberos fire engine

el camión hormigonera cement mixer
la camioneta pickup truck
la camisa shirt
la camiseta T-shirt
la camiseta interior undershirt
la campanilla bluebell
la campanilla de invierno snowdrop
el camping camping
el campo countryside
el cangrejo crab
el canguro kangaroo
cantar singing
el caracol snail
el cárdigan cardigan
cargar carrying
la carne meat
la carnicería butcher shop
la carretera road
la carretilla wheelbarrow
el carrito shopping cart
el carrito trolley
la cartera mail carrier (f)
la cartera purse
el cartero mail carrier (m)
la casa house
la cascada waterfall
el castillo castle
el castillo de arena sandcastle
catorce fourteen
la cebolla onion
la cebra zebra
el cepillo de dientes toothbrush
el cepillo del pelo hairbrush
cerca near
el cerdito piglet
el cerdo pig
el cereal cereal
las cerezas cherries
la cesta basket
el chaleco salvavidas life jacket
el champú shampoo
el charco puddle
la chimenea chimney
el chocolate chocolate
el cielo sky
cien hundred

el ciervo deer
cinco five
cincuenta fifty
el cine movie theater
el cinturón de seguridad seatbelt
la ciruela plum
el cisne swan
la ciudad town
el clavo nail (tool)
la cobija blanket
el coche car
el coche de policía police car
el coche eléctrico electric car
el cochecito stroller
la cocina kitchen
el coco coconut
el cocodrilo crocodile
el codo elbow
el cohete rocket
el cojín cushion
la col cabbage
la colina hill
los colores colors
el columpio swing
comer eating
la cometa kite
la comida food
la comisaría de policía police station
cómo how
la cómoda chest of drawers
la computadora computer
la concha shell
conducir drive
el conejillo de indias guinea pig
el conejo rabbit
confiado/confiada confident
los contrarios opposites
la corbata tie
el cordero lamb
la corona crown
correr running
las cortinas curtains
el crucero cruise ship
el cuaderno workbook
el cuadro painting
el cuadro picture

cuándo when
cuarenta forty
el cuarto de baño bathroom
el cuatriciclo quad bike
cuatro four
el cubo pail
la cuchara spoon
el cuchillo knife
el cuello neck
el cuerpo body
la curita bandage
débil weak
la decoración decorations
el dedo finger
el dedo toe
el delantal apron
delante de in front of
el delfín dolphin
dentro inside
los deportes sports
la derecha right
el desayuno breakfast
el despertador alarm clock
el destornillador screwdriver
detrás behind
el día day
dibujar drawing
diciembre December
diecinueve nineteen
dieciocho eighteen
dieciséis sixteen
diecisiete seventeen
el diente tooth
el diente de león dandelion
diez ten
el dinero money
el dinosaurio dinosaur
el disfraz costume
doce twelve
el doctor doctor (m)
la doctora doctor (f)
el dolor de barriga stomachache
el dolor de cabeza headache
domingo Sunday
dónde where
dorado/dorada gold (color)

dos two
el dragón dragon
la ducha shower
el edificio de apartamentos
   apartment building
el edredón quilt
el elefante elephant
emocionado/emocionada excited
empujar pushing
enero January
enfadado/enfadada angry
la enfermera nurse (f)
el enfermero nurse (m)
la equitación riding
escalar climbing
la escalera ladder
la escalera staircase
el escarabajo beetle
escribir writing
el escritorio desk
la escuela school
el espacio space
la espada sword
la espalda back
el espejo mirror
la esponja sponge
esquiar skiing
el estacionamiento parking lot
las estaciones seasons
el estanque pond
el estante bookshelf
el estante shelf
estar de pie standing
estar sentado sitting
estirar pulling
la estrella star
la estrella de mar starfish
el estufa stove
la excavadora digger
la fábrica factory
la falda skirt
la familia family
la farmacia drugstore
el faro lighthouse
la farola streetlight
febrero February

feliz happy
el ferry ferry
la fiebre fever
la fiesta party
el fin de semana weekend
el flamenco flamingo
las flores flowers
el flotador swim ring
el flotador salvavidas life ring
la fogata campfire
la frambuesa raspberry
el fregadero sink (kitchen)
la fresa strawberry
los frijoles beans
la fruta fruit
la fuente fountain
fuera outside
fuerte strong
la furgoneta van
el fútbol soccer
las gafas de sol sunglasses
la gallina hen
el gallo rooster
el gancho hook
el ganso goose
el garaje garage (at house)
la gasolinera gas station
gatear crawling
el gatito kitten
el gato cat
la gaviota seagull
la gimnasia gymnastics
el globo balloon
el globo aerostático hot air balloon
la golondrina swallow
la goma eraser
el gorila gorilla
la gorra cap
gracias thank you
grande big
la granja farm
el grifo faucet
gris gray
la grúa crane (machine)
los guantes gloves
los guisantes peas

la guitarra guitar
la habitación bedroom
el hada fairy
la hamaca hammock
el hámster hamster
el helado ice cream
el helicóptero helicopter
la hermana sister
el hermano brother
las herramientas tools
el hervidor kettle
el hielo ice
la hierba grass
el hipopótamo hippopotamus
la hoja leaf
el hombro shoulder
la hormiga ant
el horno oven
el hospital hospital
el hotel hotel
hoy today
las huellas animal tracks
el huevo egg
el inodoro toilet
los insectos insects
la intersección intersection
el invierno winter
la inyección shot
ir en bicicleta cycling
la izquierda left
el jabón soap
la jarra pitcher
la jirafa giraffe
el juego de magia magic set
los juegos games
jueves Thursday
jugar playing
el jugo juice
los juguetes toys
julio July
junio June
el kiwi kiwi
el koala koala
el labio lip
el ladrillo brick
el lagarto lizard

el lago lake
la lámpara lamp
los lápices de colores
    colored pencils
el lápiz pencil
la lavadora washing machine
el lavamanos sink (bathroom)
lavarse washing
la leche milk
la lechuga lettuce
leer reading
lejos far
la lengua tongue
los lentes glasses
lento/lenta slow
el león lion
el libro book
ligero/ligera light (weight)
el limón lemon
limpio/limpia clean
la linterna flashlight
el lirio lily
lleno/llena full
la lluvia rain
la luna Moon
lunes Monday
la luz light (electric)
la maceta flowerpot
la madre mother
las magdalenas cupcakes
el maíz corn
la maleta suitcase
malo/mala bad
mamá mommy
la mañana morning
mañana tomorrow
el mango mango
la manguera hose
la mano hand
la mantequilla butter
la manzana apple
el mapa map
el mar sea
la margarita daisy
la mariposa butterfly
la mariquita ladybug

marrón brown
martes Tuesday
el martillo hammer
marzo March
las mascotas pets
mayo May
la medicina medicine
la medusa jellyfish
la mejilla cheek
el melocotón peach
el melón melon
el mentón chin
el mercado market
la mermelada jam
la mesa table
los meses months
la mesita de noche bedside table
la miel honey
miércoles Wednesday
mil thousand
la mochila backpack
la mochila schoolbag
el molino windmill
el monedero coin purse
el mono monkey
la montaña mountain
morado/morada purple
la mosca fly
el mosquito mosquito
la motocicleta motorcycle
las muletas crutches
la muñeca doll
el muñeco de nieve snowman
el murciélago bat
el muro wall
el museo museum
la música music
nadar swimming
la naranja orange (fruit)
naranja orange (color)
el narciso daffodil
la nariz nose
la navegación sailing
negro/negra black
nervioso/nerviosa nervous
la niebla fog

la nieta granddaughter
el nieto grandson
la nieve snow
no no
la noche night
noventa ninety
noviembre November
las nubes clouds
nueve nine
los números numbers
la obra building site
ochenta eighty
ocho eight
octubre October
la oficina de correos post office
la oficina office
el ojo eye
la ola wave
once eleven
la oreja ear
la oruga caterpillar
oscuro/oscura dark
el osito teddy bear
el oso polar polar bear
el oso pardo brown bear
el otoño fall (season)
la oveja sheep
el padre father
los pájaros birds
la pala shovel
el palo stick
el pan bread
la panadería bakery
el panda panda
los pantalones pants
los pantalones cortos shorts
la papa potato
papá daddy
el papagayo parrot
las papas fritas french fries
el papel paper
el papél higiénico toilet paper
la papelera de reciclaje recycling bin
la parada bus stop
el paraguas umbrella

el parque park
el parque infantil playground
el pasamanos jungle gym
el pasaporte passport
el paso de cebra crosswalk
la pasta pasta
la pasta de dientes toothpaste
el pastel cake
las pastillas pills
la patineta skateboard
el patinete scooter (child's)
el patito duckling
el patito rubber duck
el pato duck
el pavo peacock
el pecho chest
el pegamento glue
el peine comb
el pelícano pelican
el pelo hair
la pelota ball
el pepino cucumber
pequeño/pequeña small
la pera pear
la percha coat hanger
el perro dog
el pescado fish (to eat)
pescar fishing
el pétalo petal
el petrolero oil tanker
el picnic picnic
el pie foot
la pierna leg
el pijama pajamas
el pimiento pepper (vegetable)
la piña pine cone
la piña pineapple
el pincel paintbrush
el pingüino penguin
el pino pine tree
las pinturas paints
el pirata pirate
la pizza pizza
el planeta planet
el plátano banana
plateado/plateada silver

el platillo saucer
el plato plate
la playa beach
la pluma pen
el pollito chick
el pollo chicken (to eat)
por favor please
por qué why
el potro foal
el prado field
la pregunta question
la prima cousin (f)
la primavera spring
el primo cousin (m)
la princesa princess
el príncipe prince
el profesor teacher (m)
la profesora teacher (f)
el puente bridge
la puerta door
la puerta de la verja gate
el puerto port
el pulgar thumb
el pulpo octopus
qué what
el queso cheese
quién who
quince fifteen
la radiografía X-ray
la raíz root
la rama branch
rápido/rápida fast
el rastrillo rake
el ratón mouse
el refrigerador refrigerator
el regalo present
la regla ruler
la reina queen
el relámpago lightning
el reloj clock
el remo oar
el rey king
el rinoceronte rhinoceros
el robot robot
la roca rock
la rodilla knee

rojo/roja red
el rompecabezas jigsaw puzzle
la ropa clothes
la rosa rose
rosa pink
ruidoso/ruidosa noisy
sábado Saturday
la sábana sheet
el saco de dormir sleeping bag
la salchicha sausage
las sandalias sandals
la sandía watermelon
el sándwich sandwich
la sangre blood
la sartén para freír frying pan
el satélite satellite
el scooter scooter (moped)
seis six
el semáforo traffic lights
la señal de tráfico road sign
septiembre September
la serpiente snake
el serrucho saw
sesenta sixty
setenta seventy
sí yes
siete seven
la silla chair
la silla de camping camping chair
la silla de playa beach chair
el sillón armchair
la sirena mermaid
sobre on
la sobrina niece
el sobrino nephew
el sofá sofa
el sol Sun
el sol sunshine
el sombrero sun hat
el sombrero de fiesta party hat
la sombrilla beach umbrella
el subibaja seesaw
el submarino submarine
sucio/sucia dirty
el suéter sweater
el supermercado supermarket

el/la surfista surfer
el suricato meerkat
la tabla de surf surfboard
el tablón board
el taburete stool
el taladro drill
el tambor drum
la tarde afternoon
la tarde evening
el taxi taxi
la taza cup
la taza mug
el tazón bowl
el tejado roof
el tejón badger
el teléfono phone
el televisor television
el tendedero clothesline
el tenedor fork
el tenis tennis
el termómetro thermometer
el ternero calf
el tesoro treasure
la tetera teapot
la tía aunt
el tiburón shark
el tiempo weather
la tienda store
la tienda de campaña tent
la Tierra Earth
el tigre tiger
las tijeras scissors
el tío uncle
el títere puppet
la toalla towel
el tobogán slide
el tomate tomato
la tormenta storm
la tortuga turtle
la tos cough
la tostada toast
el tractor tractor
tranquilo/tranquila quiet
el transporte transportation
el tranvía tram
trece thirteen

treinta thirty
el tren train
el trenecito de juguete toy train
tres three
triste sad
el tronco log
el tronco trunk (tree)
el trueno thunder
el tulipán tulip
el túnel tunnel
la uña nail (body)
el unicornio unicorn
uno/una one
las uvas grapes
la vaca cow
vacío/vacía empty
el vampiro vampire
la varita mágica magic wand
el vaso glass
veinte twenty
la vela candle
el velero sailboat
la venda dressing
la ventana window
el verano summer
verde green
las verduras vegetables
el vestido dress
el vestido de fiesta party dress
el viaje travel
el viento wind
viernes Friday
el volquete dump truck
el xilófono xylophone
el yate yacht
el yelmo helmet (medieval)
el yeso cast
el yoga yoga
el yogur yogurt
zambullirme diving
la zanahoria carrot
las zapatillas trainers
los zapatos shoes
el zorro fox

90

English/inglés–Spanish/español

afternoon la tarde
airplane el avión
airport el aeropuerto
alarm clock el despertador
ambulance la ambulancia
anchor el ancla
angry enfadado/enfadada
animal tracks las huellas
animals los animales
ant la hormiga
apartment building el edificio de apartamentos
apple la manzana
April abril
apron el delantal
arm el brazo
armchair el sillón
armoire el armario
astronaut (f) la astronauta
astronaut (m) el astronauta
athletics el atletismo
August agosto
aunt la tía
avocado el aguacate
back la espalda
backpack la mochila
bad malo/mala
badger el tejón
bakery la panadería

balcony el balcón
ball la pelota
balloon el globo
banana el plátano
bandage la curita
basket la cesta
basketball el baloncesto
bat el murciélago
bathroom el cuarto de baño
bathtub la bañera
beach la playa
beach chair la silla de playa
beach umbrella la sombrilla
beans los frijoles
bed la cama
bedroom la habitación
bedside table la mesita de noche
bee la abeja
beetle el escarabajo
behind detrás
bench el banco
bicycle la bicicleta
big grande
birds los pájaros
black negro/negra
blanket la cobija
blocks los bloques
blood la sangre
blue azul
bluebell la campanilla
blueberries los arándanos
board el tablón
body el cuerpo
book el libro
bookshelf el estante
boots las botas
bowl el tazón
branch la rama
bread el pan
breakfast el desayuno
brick el ladrillo
bridge el puente
broccoli el brócoli
brother el hermano
brown marrón
brown bear el oso pardo

bubbles las burbujas
building site la obra
bulldozer el bulldozer
buoy la boya
bus el autobús
bus stop la parada
bush el arbusto
butcher shop la carnicería
butter la mantequilla
buttercup el botón de oro
butterfly la mariposa
cabbage la col
café el café
cake el pastel
calf el ternero
campfire la fogata
camping el camping
camping chair la silla de camping
candle la vela
cap la gorra
car el coche
cardigan el cárdigan
carrot la zanahoria
carrying cargar
cast el yeso
castle el castillo
cat el gato
caterpillar la oruga
celery el apio
cement mixer el camión hormigonera
cereal el cereal
chair la silla
chameleon el camaleón
cheek la mejilla
cheese el queso
cherries las cerezas
chest el pecho
chest of drawers la cómoda
chick el pollito
chicken (to eat) el pollo
chimney la chimenea
chin el mentón
chocolate el chocolate
clean limpio/limpia

climbing escalar	**desk** el escritorio	**factory** la fábrica
clock el reloj	**digger** la excavadora	**fairy** el hada
clothes la ropa	**dinosaur** el dinosaurio	**fall (season)** el otoño
clothesline el tendedero	**dirty** sucio/sucia	**family** la familia
clouds las nubes	**diving** zambullirme	**far** lejos
coat el abrigo	**doctor (f)** la doctora	**farm** la granja
coat hanger la percha	**doctor (m)** el doctor	**fast** rápido/rápida
coconut el coco	**dog** el perro	**father** el padre
coin purse el monedero	**doll** la muñeca	**faucet** el grifo
colored pencils los lápices de colores	**dolphin** el delfín	**February** febrero
colors los colores	**donkey** el burro	**ferry** el ferry
comb el peine	**door** la puerta	**fever** la fiebre
compass la brújula	**down** abajo	**field** el prado
computer la computadora	**dragon** el dragón	**fifteen** quince
confident confiado/confiada	**drawer** el cajón	**fifty** cincuenta
corn el maíz	**drawing** dibujar	**finger** el dedo
costume el disfraz	**dress** el vestido	**fire engine** el camión de bomberos
cough la tos	**dressing** la venda	**fish (to eat)** el pescado
countryside el campo	**drill** el taladro	**fishing** pescar
cousin (f) la prima	**drinking** beber	**fishing boat** el barco de pesca
cousin (m) el primo	**drive** conducir	**five** cinco
cow la vaca	**drugstore** la farmacia	**flamingo** el flamenco
crab el cangrejo	**drum** el tambor	**flashlight** la linterna
crane (machine) la grúa	**duck** el pato	**flowerpot** la maceta
crawling gatear	**duckling** el patito	**flowers** las flores
crocodile el cocodrilo	**dump truck** el volquete	**fly** la mosca
crosswalk el paso de cebra	**eagle** el águila	**foal** el potro
crown la corona	**ear** la oreja	**fog** la niebla
cruise ship el crucero	**Earth** la Tierra	**food** la comida
crutches las muletas	**eating** comer	**foot** el pie
cucumber el pepino	**egg** el huevo	**forest** el bosque
cup la taza	**eggplant** la berenjena	**fork** el tenedor
cupcakes las magdalenas	**eight** ocho	**forty** cuarenta
curtains las cortinas	**eighteen** dieciocho	**fountain** la fuente
cushion el cojín	**eighty** ochenta	**four** cuatro
cycling ir en bicicleta	**elbow** el codo	**fourteen** catorce
daddy papá	**electric car** el coche eléctrico	**fox** el zorro
daffodil el narciso	**elephant** el elefante	**french fries** las papas fritas
daisy la margarita	**elevator** el ascensor	**Friday** viernes
dandelion el diente de león	**eleven** once	**friendly** amable
dark oscuro/oscura	**empty** vacío/vacía	**fruit** la fruta
day el día	**eraser** la goma	**frying pan** la sartén para freír
December diciembre	**evening** la tarde	**full** lleno/llena
decorations la decoración	**excited** emocionado/emocionada	**games** los juegos
deer el ciervo	**eye** el ojo	**garage (at house)** el garaje

garlic   el ajo
gas station   la gasolinera
gate   la puerta de la verja
giraffe   la jirafa
glass   el vaso
glasses   los lentes
gloves   los guantes
glue   el pegamento
goat   la cabra
gold (color)   dorado/dorada
good   bueno/buena
goodbye   adiós
goose   el ganso
gorilla   el gorila
gosling   el ansarino
granddaughter   la nieta
grandfather   el abuelo
grandmother   la abuela
grandson   el nieto
grapes   las uvas
grass   la hierba
gray   gris
green   verde
guinea pig   el conejillo de indias
guitar   la guitarra
gymnastics   la gimnasia
hair   el pelo
hairbrush   el cepillo del pelo
hammer   el martillo
hammock   la hamaca
hamster   el hámster.
hand   la mano
happy   feliz
head   la cabeza
headache   el dolor de cabeza
helicopter   el helicóptero
hello   buenos días
helmet (medieval)   el yelmo
hen   la gallina
hill   la colina
hippopotamus   el hipopótamo
honey   la miel
hook   el gancho
horse   el caballo
hose   la manguera
hospital   el hospital

hot air balloon   el globo
   aerostático
hotel   el hotel
house   la casa
how   cómo
hugging   abrazar
hundred   cien
ice   el hielo
ice cream   el helado
in front of   delante de
insects   los insectos
inside   dentro
intersection   la intersección
jam   la mermelada
January   enero
jellyfish   la medusa
jigsaw puzzle   el rompecabezas
juice   el jugo
July   julio
June   junio
jungle gym   el pasamanos
kangaroo   el canguro
kettle   el hervidor
kind   atento/atenta
king   el rey
kissing   besar
kitchen   la cocina
kite   la cometa
kitten   el gatito
kiwi   el kiwi
knee   la rodilla
knife   el cuchillo
knight   el caballero
koala   el koala
ladder   la escalera
ladybug   la mariquita
lake   el lago
lamb   el cordero
lamp   la lámpara
leaf   la hoja
left   la izquierda
leg   la pierna
lemon   el limón
lettuce   la lechuga
life jacket   el chaleco salvavidas
life ring   el flotador salvavidas

light (electric)   la luz
light (weight)   ligero/ligera
lighthouse   el faro
lightning   el relámpago
lily   el lirio
lion   el león
lip   el labio
lizard   el lagarto
log   el tronco
magic set   el juego de magia
magic wand   la varita mágica
mail carrier (f)   la cartera
mail carrier (m)   el cartero
mailbox   el buzón
mango   el mango
map   el mapa
March   marzo
market   el mercado
May   mayo
meat   la carne
medicine   la medicina
meerkat   el suricato
melon   el melón
mermaid   la sirena
milk   la leche
milkshake   el batido
mirror   el espejo
mommy   mamá
Monday   lunes
money   el dinero
monkey   el mono
months   los meses
Moon   la luna
morning   la mañana
mosquito   el mosquito
mother   la madre
motorcycle   la motocicleta
mountain   la montaña
mouse   el ratón
mouth   la boca
movie theater   el cine
mug   la taza
museum   el museo
music   la música
nail (body)   la uña
nail (tool)   el clavo

near   cerca
neck   el cuello
nephew   el sobrino
nervous   nervioso/nerviosa
niece   la sobrina
night   la noche
nine   nueve
nineteen   diecinueve
ninety   noventa
no   no
noisy   ruidoso/ruidosa
nose   la nariz
November   noviembre
numbers   los números
nurse (f)   la enfermera
nurse (m)   el enfermero
oar   el remo
October   octubre
octopus   el pulpo
office   la oficina
oil tanker   el petrolero
on   sobre
one   uno/una
onion   la cebolla
opposites   los contrarios
orange (color)   naranja
orange (fruit)   la naranja
ostrich   el avestruz
outside   fuera
oven   el horno
owl   el búho
pail   el cubo
paintbrush   el pincel
painting   el cuadro
paints   las pinturas
pajamas   el pijama
panda   el panda
pants   los pantalones
paper   el papel
park   el parque
parking lot   el estacionamiento
parrot   el papagayo
party   la fiesta
party dress   el vestido de fiesta
party hat   el sombrero de fiesta
passport   el pasaporte

pasta   la pasta
path   el camino
peas   los guisantes
peach   el melocotón
peacock   el pavo
pear   la pera
pelican   el pelícano
pen   la pluma
pencil   el lápiz
penguin   el pingüino
pepper (vegetable)   el pimiento
petal   el pétalo
pets   las mascotas
phone   el teléfono
pickup truck   la camioneta
picnic   el picnic
picture   el cuadro
pig   el cerdo
piglet   el cerdito
pillow   la almohada
pills   las pastillas
pine cone   la piña
pine tree   el pino
pineapple   la piña
pink   rosa
pirate   el pirata
pirate ship   el barco pirata
pitcher   la jarra
pizza   la pizza
planet   el planeta
plate   el plato
platform   el andén
playground   el parque infantil
playing   jugar
please   por favor
plum   la ciruela
polar bear   el oso polar
police car   el coche de policía
police officer (f)   la agente de policía
police officer (m)   el agente de policía
police station   la comisaría de policía
pond   el estanque
port   el puerto
post office   la oficina de correos

potato   la papa
present   el regalo
prince   el príncipe
princess   la princesa
puddle   el charco
pulling   estirar
pumpkin   la calabaza
puppet   el títere
puppy   el cachorro
purple   morado/morada
purse   la cartera
pushing   empujar
quad bike   el cuatriciclo
queen   la reina
question   la pregunta
quiet   tranquilo/tranquila
quilt   el edredón
rabbit   el conejo
rain   la lluvia
rainbow   el arco iris
rake   el rastrillo
raspberry   la frambuesa
reading   leer
recycling bin   la papelera de reciclaje
red   rojo/roja
refrigerator   el refrigerador
rhinoceros   el rinoceronte
rice   el arroz
riding   la equitación
right   la derecha
road   la carretera
road sign   la señal de tráfico
robot   el robot
rock   la roca
rocket   el cohete
roof   el tejado
rooster   el gallo
root   la raíz
rose   la rosa
rowboat   el bote de remos
rubber duck   el patito
rug   la alfombra
ruler   la regla
running   correr
sad   triste
sailboat   el velero

sailing   la navegación
sand   la arena
sandals   las sandalias
sandbox   el cajón de arena
sandcastle   el castillo de arena
sandwich   el sándwich
satellite   el satélite
Saturday   sábado
saucepan   la cacerola
saucer   el platillo
sausage   la salchicha
saw   el serrucho
scaffolding   el andamio
school   la escuela
school bag   la mochila
scissors   las tijeras
scooter (child's)   el patinete
scooter (moped)   el scooter
screwdriver   el destornillador
scuba diving   el buceo
sea   el mar
seagull   la gaviota
seasons   las estaciones
seat   el asiento
seatbelt   el cinturón de
   seguridad
seaweed   el alga marina
seesaw   el subibaja
September   septiembre
seven   siete
seventeen   diecisiete
seventy   setenta
shampoo   el champú
shark   el tiburón
sheep   la oveja
sheet   la sábana
shelf   el estante
shell   la concha
ship   el barco
shirt   la camisa
shoes   los zapatos
shopping bag   la bolsa de la compra
shopping cart   el carrito
short   bajito/bajita
shorts   los pantalones cortos
shot   la inyección

shoulder   el hombro
shovel   la pala
shower   la ducha
sidewalk   la acera
silver   plateado/plateada
singing   cantar
sink (bathroom)   el lavamanos
sink (kitchen)   el fregadero
sister   la hermana
sitting   estar sentado
six   seis
sixteen   dieciséis
sixty   sesenta
skateboard   la patineta
skiing   esquiar
skirt   la falda
sky   el cielo
sleeping bag   el saco de
   dormir
slide   el tobogán
slow   lento/lenta
small   pequeño/pequeña
snack bar   la cafetería
snail   el caracol
snake   la serpiente
snow   la nieve
snowdrop   la campanilla de invierno
snowman   el muñeco de nieve
soap   el jabón
soccer   el fútbol
socks   los calcetines
sofa   el sofá
space   el espacio
sponge   la esponja
spoon   la cuchara
sports   los deportes
spring   la primavera
squirrel   la ardilla
staircase   la escalera
standing   estar de pie
star   la estrella
starfish   la estrella de mar
stepping stones   el camino de
   piedras
stick   el palo
stomach   la barriga

stomachache   el dolor de
   barriga
stool   el taburete
store   la tienda
storm   la tormenta
stove   la estufa
strawberry   la fresa
stream   el arroyo
street   la calle
streetlight   la farola
stroller   el cochecito
strong   fuerte
submarine   el submarino
sugar   el azúcar
suitcase   la maleta
summer   el verano
Sun   el sol
sun hat   el sombrero
sunblock   el bloqueador
Sunday   domingo
sunglasses   las gafas de sol
sunshine   el sol
supermarket   el supermercado
surfboard   la tabla de surf
surfer   el/la surfista
swallow   la golondrina
swan   el cisne
sweater   el suéter
swim ring   el flotador
swimming   nadar
swing   el columpio
sword   la espada
T-shirt   la camiseta
table   la mesa
tall   alto/alta
taxi   el taxi
teacher (f)   el profesor
teacher (m)   la profesora
teapot   la tetera
teddy bear   el osito
television   el televisor
ten   diez
tennis   el tenis
tent   la tienda de campaña
thank you   gracias
thermometer   el termómetro

thirteen   trece
thirty   treinta
thousand   mil
three   tres
thumb   el pulgar
thunder   el trueno
Thursday   jueves
ticket   el boleto
tie   la corbata
tiger   el tigre
toast   la tostada
today   hoy
toe   el dedo
toilet   el inodoro
toilet paper   el papél higiénico
tomato   el tomate
tomorrow   mañana
tongue   la lengua
toolbox   la caja de
   herramientas
tools   las herramientas
tooth   el diente
toothbrush   el cepillo de
   dientes
toothpaste   la pasta de dientes
towel   la toalla
town   la ciudad
toy train   el trenecito de
   juguete
toys   los juguetes
tractor   el tractor
traffic lights   el semáforo
train   el tren
trainers   las zapatillas
tram   el tranvía
transportation   el transporte
trash can   el bote de basura
travel   el viaje
treasure   el tesoro
tree   el árbol
trolley   el carrito
truck   el camión
trunk (of car)   el baúl
trunk (tree)   el tronco
Tuesday   martes
tulip   el tulipán

tunnel   el túnel
turtle   la tortuga
twelve   doce
twenty   veinte
two   dos
umbrella   el paraguas
uncle   el tío
under   bajo
undershirt   la camiseta interior
unicorn   el unicornio
up   arriba
vampire   el vampiro
van   la furgoneta
vegetables   las verduras
walking   andar
wall   el muro
washing   lavarse
washing machine   la lavadora
wasp   la avispa
water   el agua
waterfall   la cascada
watermelon   la sandía
wave   la ola
weak   débil
weather   el tiempo
Wednesday   miércoles
weekend   el fin de semana
whale   la ballena
what   qué
wheelbarrow   la carretilla
when   cuándo
where   dónde
white   blanco/blanca
who   quién
why   por qué
wind   el viento
windmill   el molino
window   la ventana
winter   el invierno
witch   la bruja
woods   el bosque
workbook   el cuaderno
writing   escribir
X-ray   la radiografía
xylophone   el xilófono
yacht   el yate

yellow   amarillo/amarilla
yes   sí
yesterday   ayer
yoga   el yoga
yogurt   el yogur
zebra   la cebra
zucchini   el calabacín

**goodbye
adiós**
ah-dee<u>yoss</u>